Heritage & Hope

CHARLES WHEATLEY

Heritage and Hope: Finding My Purpose in Virgin Islands Culture
1938–1963

Books may be purchased from
Ingramspark,
1246 Heil Quaker Road
La Vergne, TN 37086
Tel 18009377978

www.ingramspark.com

Copyright © 2021 by Charles H. Wheatley

Cover and interior design by
David Ter-Avanesyan/Ter33Design

All rights reserved. No part of this book may be reproduced or used in any manner without written permission of the copyright owner except for the use of quotations in a book review. For more information, address: chwheatley58@gmail.com

First paperback edition 2021

ISBN 978-1-7378908-1-2

Heritage & Hope

FINDING MY PURPOSE *in*
VIRGIN ISLANDS CULTURE
1938–1963

CHARLES WHEATLEY

CONTENTS

ACKNOWLEDGEMENTS	6
PREFACE	7
CHAPTER ONE: *Preparation*	12
CHAPTER TWO: *Carlos's Early Life*	33
CHAPTER THREE: *Boyhood Adventures*	52
CHAPTER FOUR: *School Days*	69
CHAPTER FIVE: *Carlos and the Adults*	84
CHAPTER SIX: *Carlos and the Sea*	100
CHAPTER SEVEN: *Carlos Experiences a Hurricane*	111
CHAPTER EIGHT: *Celebrations*	125
CHAPTER NINE: *Redirecting his Life*	138
CHAPTER TEN: *Beginning Teaching*	151
CHAPTER ELEVEN: *Leaving the Enclave*	162
CHAPTER TWELVE: *Providence in Carlos's Life*	169
CHAPTER THIRTEEN: *Angels Save Carlos*	183
CHAPTER FOURTEEN: *Carlos Lives his Purpose*	193

ACKNOWLEDGEMENTS

This book could not be completed without the help and encouragement from many persons, and I hereby acknowledge those persons especially those who have been in the forefront with me on this writing journey.

First and foremost are my wife Jennie and my sons Ludwis, Lloyd and Leon. They graciously accepted all the inconveniences I put them through and I thank them for putting up with me. I also thank them for assisting me in thinking through some of my memories. I thank my grandchildren who have been a source of inspiration to me, and my siblings who provided opportunities for some of the experiences recorded herein.

My life has been influenced positively by many voices of love, kindness, hope, promise, confidence, inspiration, and humility and I thank all these persons for their influence, inspiration, and encouragement.

Those relatives, colleagues, and friends who read the manuscript and gave me valuable advice in shaping this story, I thank them. Among them are Edgar Leonard, Lisa Penn-Lettsome, Cassanda Titley-O'Neal, Winston King, and John Wesley Forbes who permitted me to include their reviews in this publication.

Finally, I thank my editor, Howard Lovy, my book designer, David Ter-Avanesyan, and artist Reuben Vanterpool for their invaluable contributions to the quality of this book.

PREFACE

Carlos woke up on a bright Monday morning, stood drowsily by his window, and looked outside for five minutes, breathing the fresh tropical breeze.

"Today I will celebrate the beginning of a journey which I was planning and preparing for during the last six years," he shouted without any warning.

Carlos wanted to record the story of the first twenty-five years in the British Virgin Islands. He decided to record it for his children, grandchildren, great-grandchildren, other relatives and friends, as well as other readers. He was anxious to tell other people how the Lord led him through the culture and life in the British Virgin Islands during the middle decades of the twentieth century. As he experienced life in that culture, he believed God had been preparing him for a special purpose since his conception.

During his first twenty-five years, he encountered a few people who assisted him in one way or another in making life meaningful for him. He remembered the love shown by those people and their words of encouragement that helped him to face some of the darkest battles he encountered along life's highway. The simplicity, humility and integrity shown by these people had an indelible effect on his life. He had a burning interest in the quality of the environment in which he grew up. He learned to be a percipient and thrifty young man while the people in his neighborhood went about their daily work cheerfully and diligently.

His mother was hard-working and cheerful, and she left a permanent love for work in her will for him. All her children called her Ma as a pet name because she was a firm manager, and that name became one of her identifications in the enclave where she lived.

As a young boy he used to listen fervently and attentively to the stories his mother told him about his birth. She was very happy that she was going to be a mother. One day, her best friend offered her a naseberry, a fruit she disliked but she took it to satisfy her friend. While taking it, she scratched the inside of her right ring finger with her right thumb. When Carlos was born, he had the mark of a naseberry on the inside of his right ring finger, just where his mother scratched her finger. Carlos has prized this naseberry mark on his finger to this day.

She told him that she went to the hospital in a sailboat because there were no passenger ferries or taxis available. When she arrived at the hospital there wasn't a vacant bed, so she had to sit in an easy chair during labor. A few minutes before Carlos was born the matron took her to a bed. Everyone in the hospital visited him because he had an unusual head of curly hair and dark sideburns.

He spent eight days in the hospital and then his mother took him to her home with her foster parents. They loved Carlos dearly and cared for him carefully and faithfully every day. And he grew to love his foster grandmother, Mahitabel, dearly. After his mother moved to her home, she would carry him to spend days with his foster grandmother. Sometimes he would sleep over and return home to his mother on the following day.

As soon as Carlos was able to speak, his mother taught him to pray. She had a strong belief in God and prayed every day for guidance and protection. She believed that God guided people to do things right but Satan, the evil one, always discouraged them from doing things right. The first prayers Carlos had to memorize were:

1. *Gentle Jesus meek and mild,*
   Look upon a little child,

Pity my simplicity.
Suffer me to come to Thee.

2. *Now I lay me down to sleep,*
   I pray The Lord my soul to keep.
   If I should die before I wake.
   I pray The Lord my soul to take.

3. *Mathew, Mark, Luke and John*
   Bless the bed that I lay on.
   Four corners have my bed,
   Four angels at my head,
   One to sing one to play,
   Two to take my soul away.

If Carlos went to bed before praying, his mother would wake him up if he had fallen asleep and insist that he repeated his prayers. This was the beginning of his prayer life, which grew stronger and stronger with time. He became very conscious of being watched by God every second of the day. That consciousness has remained an important part of his life, from childhood to adulthood.

As Carlos grew into boyhood and adolescence, he would tell his friends that God was watching his character, his conduct, and his conversations but most of his friends dismissed him when he raised the subject. He believed that God had created him for a special Purpose, and he was responsible for discovering that special Purpose. He loved to serve other people, was gentle and kind to others and always wanted to help those who were experiencing difficulties in performing their work in the village and at school.

He was torn by two influences for many years. One of these influences pressured him to satisfy his physical needs and put all his energy in doing so. The other influence was deeper within him and challenged him to put his faith in God, who controlled the universe. He wrestled with these two influences, did a lot of research and reading to help him to cope with the struggle. The book *The Road to Character*, by David Brooks, provided some valuable insights to his struggle. He also read *The Lonely Man of Faith*, by Rabbi Joseph B. Soloveitchik. These two books described a deeper struggle within himself. They also illustrated how he harmonized his actions while living in this capitalistic world with the promises of a better world after death. The following excerpt illustrate that enlightenment:

> *Recently I've been thinking about the difference between the resume' virtues and the eulogy virtues. The resume' virtues are the ones you can list on your resume', the skills that you bring to the job market and that contribute to external success. The eulogy virtues are deeper. They are the virtues that get talked about at your funeral, the ones that exist at the core of your being-whether you are kind, brave, honest or faithful; what kind of relationships you formed. (The Road to Character, p. ix).*

Carlos has been thankful for the rich heritage from which he emerged, grew, and was groomed. That heritage was the shared memory, the lived experiences and the stories of several generations of enslaved black people and their liberated descendants. The traditions, beliefs, and values that constitute this shared memory, lived experiences and stories, when woven together into the tapestry of his heritage, have created an environment where his endowments by God have been nurtured, blossomed, and grown for the benefit of humankind.

In the following pages, Carlos shows how his upbringing and the culture of the British Virgin Islands influenced the search for his Purpose of service to humankind.

CHAPTER ONE
The Preparation

"Nothing stamped with the Divine image and likeness was sent into the world to be trodden on and degraded and imbruted by its fellows." —**Abraham Lincoln**

Carlos had a burning desire for many years to write a memoir of his life. He thought about writing it while he was in elementary school and had to learn how to write stories and essays. He thought about this project day after day and night after night. Sometimes he would sit down for several hours and write pages about the things he had been doing, the things he had seen, the things he had heard, the places he went, and so on. After putting in all that time on his dream book, he would tear up what he had written and feed the fire with it.

This weekend, he felt restless, and the only thing that would satisfy him was to write. He spent almost the whole weekend writing, and after putting all his ideas on paper, he felt disappointed about what he had written. He did not develop a plan to guide him; he had written down the episodes and stories just as he remembered them. As usual, his weekend work was thrown in the fire.

As the fire consumed the paper, a dreadful thought came to him. Was he burning up the knowledge he had gained through life? He looked at the embers as the wind blew them over the yard. He remembered a line from a passage he had studied. It read something like this, "the chaff which the wind blows away." (Psalm 1:4). It dug deep into his inner self. That was a turning point in preparing him to write a memoir of the first twenty-five years of his life.

He wanted to write this memoir for two reasons. First, he wanted to produce a record of his activities from childhood to adolescence for his children, grandchildren, great-grandchildren, other relatives, and friends, and acquaintances. Carlos was inspired to write this book urgently because the oral tradition he knew was disappearing rapidly. It had been eroded through resistance and rejection by younger generations who were only motivated by current activities. Oral tradition was one of several cultural traits and characteristics that were lying on their death beds. A few cultural traits that faced a similar fate were:

1. Greeting other people as a courtesy.
2. Parents teaching children to pray and read the Bible.
3. Sharing possessions in neighborly love.

In order to better understand what he meant by oral tradition, Carlos decided to take you to the enclave where he lived and to share his views. During the period covered by this memoir, oral tradition was revered. People used that medium to keep in touch with the past, inform the present, and provide some guidance for the future. The people in the enclave where Carlos lived also paid special attention to the importance of daily discourse. They indulged in the current community narratives, analytically looking at them through the lens of their personal narratives and their personal experiences. They would spin the popular narratives to make them fit into their personal ones. Within these narratives, he perceived some interesting themes, including populism, nativism, and protectionism.

The populists tried to control the loyalty of other people so that their influences would grow as they gained the respect and support of other people. The children also practiced the same principle in their play so that it became a part of growing-up behavior that helped to shape their lives. An example of the effect of a populist narrative can be seen in the following episode.

Many decades ago, a man by the name of Harry inflicted severe wounds on a woman whom he meant to kill with his cutlass. After committing the crime, he mounted his horse hurriedly and rode swiftly through the street, an unusual pattern of behavior. On seeing him moving so fast, people asked him why he was riding so fast, and the narrative said he replied, "You will hear." That response was interwoven in the local narrative. People used the phrase, "Harry said, 'you will hear'" when they believed that the truth of a situation would be made known in the future.

The inhabitants of the enclave also believed in nativism. They discussed the importance of protecting the interests of their forebears for future generations and preserving them against foreign infiltration. The older generations prized their possessions, especially their landholdings. They believed that possession was their birthright and would never part with it under normal circumstances. They would go hungry but hold onto their land and endure the effects of poverty while being rich in possessions. According to the way many of them spoke, they seemed to believe their land was an extension of themselves, which they would never sell. Carlos had seen that "sacred belief"—the internalization of land ownership—change with passing decades as the territory moved from an agricultural to a service-oriented economy. People were no longer as close to the land as their forebears were because they did not work it to produce food. With this change, people had lost the joy of seeing the land yield its store of food in fruits, vegetables, and meats, which were staples for the dinner table of their forebears.

Since the restoration of the local Legislative Council in 1950, populism began to creep into the enclave and the wider community. During the 1940s, the United States built a naval station next door on St. Thomas. Hundreds of British Virgin Islanders migrated there to work. This continued through the duration of World War II. After the war ended, most of these people returned home, along with others who had migrated to Puerto Rico, the Dominican Republic, Cuba, and Aruba in search of work. These returning citizens brought back new ideas, knowledge, and skills, and began to awaken and energize Virgin Islanders to agitate for better government and better living conditions.

They were discontented with the lack of secondary education in the Virgin Islands, inadequate medical services, poor management of the Public Works Department, among other grievances. This discontent culminated with an assembly on the Old Recreation Grounds in Road Town, where dissidents conducted a religious service and then marched through Road Town to Government House (called Olympus by the people) where the commissioner (head of the government) lived and delivered a petition from the people. Here is an excerpt from that petition:

> *We the people of the British Virgin Islands, theoretically a free people by reason of the fact that we are supposed to be British Subjects and Citizens of the British Empire, are today in numbers assembled as a Demonstration of Protest against certain conditions under which we have hitherto been forced to live. . . . One of the purposes of this Demonstration today is for us to achieve a measure of political freedom for ourselves and generations of the future. (Harrigan and Varlack, The Virgin Islands Story, 1975, p.158).*

This was a turning point in the governance of the Virgin Islands. In July of the following year (1950), the General Legislative Council of the British Virgin Islands was restored and inaugurated on December 5, 1950, after being abolished in 1902.

People began to organize in groups and oppose one another in order to gain power and influence. The emergence of political parties introduced organized divisions, which was not a characteristic of the community. The groupings within the community also expanded to the religious life of the inhabitants. Historically, there were two denominations—Methodist and Anglican—which introduced Christianity and education to the emancipated black people during the first half of the nineteenth century. New groupings along religion developed, and these helped to enhance the power of populism in the British Virgin Islands community.

That populist movement also weakened the protectionism of the older generation, and so land became a commodity on the market. Many families sold their birthright, which their forebears had fought to preserve. In this move to get rid of their land, nativism also went out with the "bathwater." The longstanding inhabitants began to lose the control they had over their home country. They were becoming "hewers of stones and drawers of water" in their homeland.

Carlos also observed that the people who lived during this period despised the trades by which they lived. They would tell their children to do their schoolwork so that they would not have to work like them as shipwrights, carpenters, masons, fishermen, and farmers. They wanted their children to work for other people in offices rather than being entrepreneurs like their parents. These adults really believed that what they were laboring for—an honest, decent living—was inferior in status to working as a clerk in government or teaching in a school. Those who worked with the hook, hoe, hammer, and trowel were inferior to those who sat at a typewriter and wrote with a pen at a desk.

Another trait that Carlos perceived and disliked included attitudes toward skin color and the type of hair on one's head. Those people, many of them called mulatto in those days, who were descended from Caucasian and African ancestry, were considered superior because they had "white blood" in their veins. That prejudice divided families and communities and was prevalent in the enclave. In a family, one could find children of the same parents with skin color ranging from very fair to very dark. What was also noticeable: the fairer ones would identify the darker ones by denigrating names such as "black boy," "black face," "black monkey," "black head." In a sibling rivalry, it was one of the elements of the argument that generated heated antagonism from the darker siblings. Carlos lived between two communities where this struggle existed. The residents of Community A were mainly of Caucasian and Black ancestry. They were well-educated and highly skilled people. The residents of Community B were farmers and descendants of enslaved Africans. The feeling of inferiority was further reinforced because people from Community B had to go to Community A to attend school and church, pay their taxes, get married, and sell their produce. Government agents resided in Community A. However, the advent of automobiles, emigration to the US Virgin Islands, as well as an awakening of the inner self of the residents in Community B changed that attitude significantly, but with clearer lines of separation and independence. The separation was represented in political district alignment and representation, educational institutions, health clinics, places of divine worship, entrepreneurial activities, outstanding scholarship, community services, and recreational facilities in each community. The situation has changed to unity within difference.

He also noticed that the emphasis on reading good books was being challenged by the television and telephone. The fleeting but appealing nature of most of the content in television shows robbed the individual of the love for reading, and it also limited their capacities for writing continuous prose and poetry. The technology limited the literary and creative imagination and expression of British Virgin Islanders. In this culture, young people have been gradually changing as their British Virgin Islands identity continued to be eroded through the narratives of the day and by the behaviors displayed on the stage of life. Some of the ingredients of this identity were land rights, descent, family reputation, caring for one another, respect for senior people, obedience to other people, and a livelihood from hard work. This identity erosion was partly the result of metropolitan characteristics that had infiltrated the agricultural community. Those characteristics included diversity in race, ethnicity, economic status, education, religion, and nationality.

Today, in this small community of sixty square miles, there are more than 120 different nationalities. Many young people have been searching earnestly to discover who they really are because the cultural gulf between children and their parents and grandparents is widening rapidly. On the other hand, many of these young people willfully denied the cultural, social, and economic experiences which constituted the building blocks of their existence. Carlos firmly believed that individuals are the product of life's circumstances-good and/or bad-and everyone should take some time to reflect on who she or he has become. Such reflection could help everyone become better grounded in today's turbulent environment. This memoir is intended to help identify the roots of this present society and how they have shaped Carlos's life and helped him to discover his purpose in life.

His urgency behind the writing of this memoir is also grounded in another loss within the territory. The peace and tranquility that have characterized the British Virgin Islands for the first half of the last century are gradually being chipped away. This cultural change was driven by various influences from the demographic changes which have been gradually taking place in the Territory, and the affluence spun off from the evolution of a service economy that had despised the agricultural economy of the first half of the twentieth century. Cradled within this cultural change sat territorial authority driven and nourished by worldly success with characteristics such as self-reliance, self-control, resilience, self-expression, self-liberalism, and tenacity. At the same time, the culture that Carlos's forebears lived included loyalty to their superiors, employers, their coworkers and neighbors, their parents, their siblings, and all the others with whom they associated, a culture of self-effacement, self-combat, selflessness, generosity, and self-sacrifice has been fading away like stars in the morning. Amid this cultural upheaval, British Virgin Islanders wander around trying to unmask, to understand, to clarify, to represent, and defend who they are as individuals and as a community of individuals. He was convinced that his people need to step back a little, stop defining truth by power and influence and build their lives on a genuine sense of human dignity and a just and inclusive social order that acknowledges that all human beings are God's creation.

Carlos lived inside the tensions between the voices of hope and the voices of despair. These voices spoke in various tones, reflecting the attitudes of the people in his neighborhood. One day he was very upset by the utterance of one of those voices, so he ran home and commanded his mother's attention immediately.

She became concerned at his appearance and asked him, "What is the matter with you?"

"Ma" Carlos answered. "That woman just told me she will see to it that I do not become anything in life."

"What did you do to her?" asked his mother.

"Nothing," said Carlos.

"Sit down and listen to me, Carlos," demanded his mother.

"There are all kinds of people in this world, and they will behave differently," she told him. "They do not think alike, neither do they love people alike. Because of these differences in behavior, you must learn to listen and do not listen, to hear and do not hear. By that, I mean you do not allow what other people say to upset you."

"But what caused her to make that statement?" Carlos asked his mother.

"Maybe she was upset about something or with someone, and she expressed her feelings on you," his mother told him, hoping to get his mind off the remark.

Carlos never forgot that remark, and he always watched that woman with caution. Apart from isolated incidents like that one, he had experienced large amounts of positive advice and counsel from many people who helped to guide him through life. The voices of those people have taught him how to serve others selflessly. He saw those people rendering service to their neighbors willingly. Those people have left an indelible effect on his first twenty-five years, and so he decided to give them special mention. He placed those voices into seven groups so that he could remember them with greater ease. They have become part of his oxygen.

In a broader context, they would be classified as unsung heroes and their names may not appear in any publication as a testimony to their contributions to the development of the British Virgin Islands. They helped to keep the community alive through their entrepreneurial activities; they could feel proud for the civic services which they rendered free of charge, their caring eyes and hands, and most of all the exemplary behavior they demonstrated for young people like Carlos. This feeble mention of those stalwarts cannot do them justice, but at least some of their descendants could feel proud to know that someone acknowledged something their forebears had done for humankind.

The contributions of those voices helped Carlos to face many dark forces he encountered during this portion of his life's journey, to build his character, guide his conduct, and manage his conversations. Many of those voices were lighthouses on his journey. He had escaped many human-created rocks and reefs and withstood many bitter and sweet episodes of life because those people cared enough about him to give him wise counsels and rebuke him when the occasions warranted such.

Although they have passed on to their eternal rest, Carlos felt so inspired by them that he decided to acknowledge their contributions to his life because, for him, they would never die. He had been blessed to have met those humble, loving, industrious, generous, thoughtful, positive, and caring people. They lived across the Anegada to Jost Van Dyke, and across Tortola, East End to West End. Their voices have continued to whisper in his ears from day to day, reminding him of their past relationships. During such times, he could feel power coming from their personalities. It was the power of their internal struggles with their sins and their search for deliverance and self-respect. Whenever he thought about them, he was encouraged by their accomplishments. They acknowledged that as human beings, we were flawed with weaknesses, but if we were aware of these weaknesses, we could practice a mode of living that would help us to overcome them. These people have contributed to the development of the British Virgin Islands through their investments in the lives of other people. They have instilled a sense of national pride, of belonging to the British Virgin Islands, of community love, of civic duty, which propelled Carlos to continue his service to humankind.

Whenever he tried to minimize his availability for service, the True Self within him reminded him that he had not yet fulfilled his purpose in life, so he needed to continue serving. Carlos continued to be inspired and energized by those fond memories, which increased his love for humankind. It is this love that drove him to share these memories, hoping that some needy brother or sister, some individual battered by life's brutal forces, some weary and discouraged soul would be encouraged to face life more courageously and confidently, and to find new hope for the future. Perhaps a spark from reading this book may ignite that love for humankind that already abided in their hearts.

Carlos grew up in James Young, an enclave of East End, Tortola, British Virgin Islands. It is situated at the foot of James Young Hill, which is owned by the residents of the enclave and forms its northern boundary. On the eastern end, the enclave is bounded by the trajectory of Tarris Hill ravine, which separates Tarris Hill estate from the enclave. On the western end, the enclave is bounded by the trajectory of James Young ravine, which separates it from Major Bay estate. On the south, the enclave meets the blue Caribbean Sea. Several maritime activities took place in what is known as James Young Bay. During the period of this memoir, fishermen brought fish to market, put their boats on dry dock, cleaned and repaired them as needed. Sailors who traveled to other Caribbean Islands embarked and disembarked in the bay. Exports and imports move in and out regularly, and people congregated on the Bay for commercial reasons as the boats took off and returned from trips abroad.

The enclave has been dominated by two families-the Wheatleys and the Chalwells. The Wheatleys, who originally came from Anegada, married the Chalwells who came from Old Plantation and Greenland on Tortola. These two families intermarried to such an extent that most of the residents in the enclave are blood relatives. There were also members from other families who moved to the enclave through marriage. Other characteristics of the population in the enclave mirrored the wider community of the eastern end of Tortola. There were agriculturalists, fishermen, boat builders, carpenters, sailors, teachers, nurses, musicians, preachers, churchgoers, workers in cottage industries like making straw hats and bags, other craftsmen, entrepreneurs including shopkeepers and bakers.

Carlos's parents devoted more than an hour sometimes in the evening, sharing their life stories with him and his siblings. Through those stories, he and his siblings were connected to their relatives throughout the Territory. His parents told them about their childhood years and their school days. They told them jumbie stories, treasure stories, biblical stories, horror stories, tall tales, and love stories. A typical evening storytime would begin with his mother singing one of the songs she learned at school or one of the hymns she learned in Sunday school. She also loved to sing those English, and Scottish folk songs like: *The Highland of Scotland, Milly Molly, Begone Dull Care*, and the list goes on. She never sang a Caribbean or a Virgin Islands folksong on these occasions, but in unguarded moments when she was alone, he would hear her singing one of them now and then. If he encroached on her space, she would stop singing abruptly. Later, Carlos found out the reason for her not singing them during storytime was she thought the lyrics were too vulgar. Here is a short excerpt from one of those Virgin Islands folksongs:

> *Dorothy went to bathe,*
> *Dorothy loses her way,*
> *She cried out laud, laud,*
> *Fire in de water.*

These songs were tabooed by the religious people of the community. Carlos used to enjoy her stories because she took him to Salt Island, the place where she lived with her parents.

During her early years on Salt Island, she learned to fish, harvest whelks, dive conchs along the bay, reap salt from the salt ponds, swim like a fish, row like a boy, but most of all to be friendly and kind to other people especially strangers. Her mother taught her to cook, wash clothes, and how to perform all the relevant household chores. His mother insisted from an early age that he learned to perform those duties even though it was not proper for a boy to be seen doing some of those things, especially cooking. Her parting stories with life on Salt Island captured Carlos's attention. As she told her story of being uprooted from the island of her birth, she reminded him that all the island's children experienced the same fate. They were placed in selected homes across the islands of Tortola and Virgin Gorda to attend school. There was no school on Salt Island except for a very short period in 1837, when the Anglicans opened a small school. In that same year, the school was destroyed by a hurricane and it was not rebuilt. She was torn from her Salt Island playmates—some she never saw again until they were adults.

This uprooted little girl destined to be Carlos's mother was transplanted in East End, Tortola, where she was immersed in the culture of that community. She soon found new friends at school and in the village as she started a new life. She used to brag to Carlos about her extraordinary achievements at school, excelling beyond most of her friends. She loved the opportunities those results afforded her to help her friends with their school assignments. She told Carlos how they had to write on a small slab of slate because composition books were scarce, and many parents could not afford to buy these books for their children. In any case, a student spent the first two years of schooling writing on a slate. This requirement was still in force when Carlos attended elementary school. What a long journey from the slate to today's iPad! Andy's mother's "iPad" was her slate, and so was Carlos's, even though he completed the journey from the slate to the iPad.

As his mother related her stories to him, the tone of her voice, though friendly, seemed to indicate that she expected him to perform as she did at school. Now and then, she would challenge him to surpass her record. She commanded a handwriting *par excellence*. It was like a craft that she perfected every time she put pen to paper. Carlos confessed many times that he envied her handwriting and tried desperately to equal or surpass it. He practiced writing every day, changing the style of his lettering until he was satisfied with his accomplishments. He never reached her standard, but through perseverance, he attained an admirable level of competence.

He was very excited about two stories and he decided to share them with his friends. The first story tells about the adventure of digging for treasure and was passed on by oral tradition and the other story witnessed by Carlos talks about the encounter with a jumbie riding a donkey:

The Snake with the Gold Teeth

The treasure associated with this story was buried on the island of Great Camanoe and was no secret among the people at the eastern end of Tortola. Many people tried to unearth this treasure but were unsuccessful. All the treasure hunters claimed that they saw the chest with the treasure and at the sight of the iron chest, a large snake pushed his head up and opened his mouth wide. At that point, everyone fled but took enough time to observe that the snake's mouth had gold teeth. After several expeditions failed to get the treasure, people stop trying to get it. One night, Mr. Fox dreamt that a man offered him the treasure. The man instructed him how to approach the site and who should accompany him. He was told to carry a mirror along with the equipment for digging the treasure, and when the snake showed its head and opened its mouth, Mr. Fox would hold the mirror in front of the snake. When the snake has seen himself in the mirror, he would disappear, and the treasure can be taken without any difficulty. Mr. Fox was so elated the next morning that he shared his dream with many of his friends. Everyone encouraged him to do exactly what the man in the dream told him, otherwise he would not get the treasure. He got busy and made all the preparations for the expedition without any delay. The evening arrived and the hunting party rowed the boat from Tortola to Great Camanoe. The weather was perfect, a cool easterly trade wind and the moon was shining brightly in a cloudless sky. They arrived at Great Camanoe and moored the boat close enough to the shore so that they could disembark easily. They collected their tools and the mirror and moved to the site of the treasure. The journey from the boat to the site was filled with obstacles, big stones, fallen branches, and insects with venomous lances enjoying the tranquility of their environment. The group arrived unharmed at the site. Everything moved as planned. However, there was an eerie feeling in the air, a feeling that some exciting thing was about to happen. Everyone was anxious, each heart beating at a terrific speed. In the heads of these treasure seekers, ideas for using this treasure began to surface. They were all beginning to think about their plans for the treasure.

They started to dig. The pickaxes struck stone after stone and sometimes sparks flew from the impact of the pickaxes. Beads of perspiration ran down their cheeks and watered the earth as they piled it at the mouth of the excavation. At last, the pickaxes struck the chest with the treasure. A sigh of relief filled their hearts. Without losing any time, they cleared away the loose earth to make sure that they had really seen the prize. Their hearts pumped blood faster than usual and they breathed heavily to make sure there was enough oxygen in their blood. The human voice was reduced to a whisper as the toil progressed. Everything proceeded as planned without commands. Even the natural population must have wondered if the heavens were falling in as the pickaxes dug deep into the earth. Their expectations turned into subdued as the pickaxes struck the iron chest with the prize. They removed the loose earth very quickly to confirm that they had seen the prize. Just as they were about to grab the chest, the snake showed its head and opened its mouth wide. Fright mingled with fear canceled their better judgments and they forgot the mirror. Without hesitating, they fled to the boat like Bolt in the Olympics, leaving all their tools and the mirror behind. Their destination was the anchored boat in the bay. They claimed that the snake followed them to the shore. On reaching the shore, they jumped into the sea, clamored on board their boat and rowed home exhausted and disappointed. Their failure made good gossip of which they became the objects. The enclave was ablaze with the news the following morning.

A Jumbie riding a Donkey

A jumbie, in the Virgin Islands, is a bad (evil) spirit of the dead that appears in human form. It may enter the house or walk around it, stealing the voice of a living person. If a Jumbie calls your name, do not answer or you will die soon after. Jumbie stories have secured a favored place in the narratives of the community for generations. Carlos heard some hair-raising stories which kept him awake at night. Before there were streetlights and motorable roads, when the narrow paths were used for walking and horse or donkey riding, jumbies were plentiful. Almost every week, you would hear a story or two about jumbie activities.

A certain popular man died. He was known for riding a donkey every day to and from his farm. He loved to smoke a tobacco pipe as he sat on his donkey day after day with both legs hanging on the same side. The local people referred to this style of riding as "riding woman fashion." One evening, months after his death, Carlos had to run an errand for his mother after twilight. It was about eight o'clock in the evening and there was no moonlight and all around was very dark. It was so dark that he could not see the road before him. He was walking by faith. Suddenly, an eerie feeling came over his body, and fear seized him. In the distance, before him, he saw an image of the same man on his donkey with his pipe in his mouth riding towards him. He remembered the belief in the community that a jumbie would not disappear if you keep your eyes on it. He decided to do just that as he approached the oncoming image. His hair raised up on his head like the hair on a dog's back when he is about to attack prey, his eyes watered, and his heartbeat increased, but he kept his gaze. Fear had disappeared; he wanted to see what would happen when they met. He felt as if he was in a different world, but he kept his gaze. He did not wink even though his sight was blurred with tears. When he got within a few yards of the jumbie, he could not hold out any longer, and he winked. When he opened his eyes, there was no donkey and no man. He looked around to be sure that the donkey did not turn aside, but he saw nothing. Fear seized him again, and he started running as fast as he could. He outran every animal he met on his way and did not stop until he reached home. He may have outrun his guardian angel, who seized with wonder tried to protect him and did not stop until he reached home. He told his mother and the others at home what had happened. When the sages in the community heard his story, they warned him not to do that again. They told him if he did not wink, the jumbie would have slapped him. He never attempted that feat again.

Two things caught Carlos's attention from all the stories he heard and experienced. The first was the human side, the things and actions in which he was immersed every day. This he could see and understand. The second was the spiritual side. There was always an invisible character he could not fully identify. As he grew older, the presence of this character influenced his life until he understood his purpose in life.

Many of his friends did not have the opportunity to learn from their mothers' teaching in the way Carlos was able to learn. After working all day in the fields, sowing and reaping agricultural produce, then returning home to prepare the evening meal, those mothers did not have the time to spend with their children before retiring at night. Carlos tried to emulate his mother and spent many hours helping some of his schoolmates to learn basic skills in grammar and mathematics. Giving that assistance became a habit that almost enslaved him. Many of those classmates demanded more time than he could afford, but he could not refuse because they threatened him if he refused to assist them. His freedom came when he was promoted to a higher grade leaving many of them behind. It was a sorry-glad moment in his life. After that episode, he was very careful to control his relationships with his schoolmates.

Being the first of twelve children, Carlos was given certain responsibilities at home. He thought that he was a little "chief" with some "Indians."

He was big brother, oldest brother, senior brother, boss brother, defender of the clan, titles that pumped him up to assert his authority of caring for his siblings. He felt a sense of responsibility for setting a good example for them. Whenever he played father and punished anyone of them, the whole clan would challenge his authority with a kind of fearful opposition. If they rebelled against him too forcefully, they could very well end up before the parental judges. If that happened, the verdict could have been a stern, piercing rebuke, the denial of a privilege, assignment of additional work for a specified period, or make an apology to big brother. The fallout from these episodes was short-lived but helped to cement relationships among one another.

Carlos's parents did not have much. They had to work very hard to keep food on the table and to meet the growing needs of their children. As the children grew up, the older ones assisted in providing for the family. The need to do this was reinforced when Carlos's father died suddenly while he was still a young teenager. This was a turning point in his life as he felt obliged to fill the role of his deceased father in the family. It was a very tall order, a challenging position in an agrarian subsistence economy where jobs were scarce and wages were extremely low. It was a situation where every member of the family played an important role in keeping the family together. Shortly after his father's death, the Methodist church offered him a position as a pupil-teacher-the modern equivalent would be a teacher's assistant—for a meager salary of $16.67 per month. This would help you to understand what he meant by low or meager wages.

To make life more difficult in the enclave, many of the residents were unfriendly and unkind to his family. The families were very closely knitted together, but their behavior was not always positive. In fact, as children, his parents would caution them about some of the neighbors. Relationships appeared to be warm on the surface but cold beneath that surface. There were elements of hatred, bad-mind, envy, resistance, and power struggle floating around. "Crabantics" was popular. His parents spent a lot of time weekly instructing him how to navigate through these influences and attributes, and not indulge in practicing any of them.

The influences in the enclave were mixed. The hunger for external things, material possessions, was strong, and that motivated some people to use any means to get what they wanted, not necessarily what they needed. Many of them did so honestly, but others paid little attention to morality, especially if the moral code did not match their aspirations. Carlos told a story about his grandfather, from whom he received wise counsel very often. That story tells of a strange man from another island who appeared in the community. The news spread very quickly that he was a necromancer and people avoided him as the devil runs from holy water. Carlos was surprised that this man became a fishing partner with his father and grandfather. They worked together for some time but not without criticism from the community. People warned his grandfather about this association and encouraged him to break it up. He refused to listen to his friends and relatives. One fishing day, this man did not turn up to go fishing, neither did he inform his grandfather that he was not going on that trip. Carlos's father and grandfather went to pull the fish traps. In the middle of the operation, his grandfather collapsed, speechless and paralyzed, in the boat. He was rushed to the hospital but died within hours. The medical report indicated a massive heart attack and stroke were the causes of death. People believed the report until this strange man claimed openly that he engineered the death by using his necromantic powers because his grandfather's fish traps would always catch more fish than his. This is a strange story, but it illustrates a typical influence of the day. How would a fourteen-year-old teenager respond to stories like this? Carlos explained how one of his close friends told him that he came upon a pot on three legs filled with stuff and boiling without any fire. In his fright, the friend ran shouting and calling others to witness this phenomenon. Out of the blue, Mr. Bonjou, a senior citizen, appeared in front of him and threatened him if he did not keep his mouth shut. Carlos had to learn how to guide his siblings and himself along with the help of his mother through many difficult and challenging experiences.

One of the challenging experiences for his family was the fact that most of the people in the enclave considered his mother an outsider because she hailed from Salt Island. She came from what they called "the Cay" to live among Tortolans—the name for born residents of Tortola. "Cay people" were considered lower in social rank than Tortolans. Carlos's mother asserted her claim to the enclave through marriage and come "hell or high water" she was not relinquishing that claim to any of the neighbors. Her determination set the tone for her relationships. She was determined to raise her children without being submerged by the attitudes and behaviors of that little community. On many occasions, Carlos would listen to the strains of her struggles, her trials, and her triumphs and would see the tears and sweat roll down her cheeks, symbolizing the agony of rejection and family pressure. During those times, he would inhale the essence of her daily life beneath the strife and struggle and digest her teachings. He characterized his mother in the following paraphrased passage:

"She used her voice for kindness, her eyes for compassion, her hands for charity, her mind for truth, and her heart for love."

That is the legacy that he inherited from his mother, a legacy that would be the wind under his wings as he ascends the heights ahead.

Carlos was not claiming that everything his mother did was perfect. She had a "hot" tongue, and anyone who provoked that fire would quickly understand what "salt butter cost a pound." That tongue kept the neighbors at bay and reinforced the hatred, envy, and rejection within the enclave. She had many friends outside the enclave and few within it. She was a merry bird, chirping, and singing as she plowed her way through the vicissitudes of life.

As you read this memoir, you will get a glimpse into British Virgin Islands culture during the mid-decades of the twentieth century. You will also gain some insight into the challenges of young people and children who lived through those years. Within that culture, Carlos was born, lived, played with friends, walked over hills, through valleys, cared for cows and goats, collected dry wood for the oven and fireplace, sold fish, sold straw hats and bags, cut timbers to the Tortola boat, groomed vegetable gardens on the hillside, swam with friends, played water sports, learned to somersault in water, dived conchs and lobsters, harvested whelks, draw water from wells, attended school, worshiped God, rendered service to those in need and refused to emigrate to another country in search of a better life, but rather "suffered the afflictions of his people" and helped to improve the community in which he lived. Join with Carlos as he takes you into the memories of yesterday.

CHAPTER TWO
Carlos's Early Life

"Never allow someone to be your priority while allowing yourself to be their option." — **Mark Twain**

Carlos and his father sat together chatting when he suddenly said, "Daddy, where is Ma?"

"She has gone to the hospital," his father replied.

That made no sense to Carlos because he did not know what a hospital was. He continued to question his father until he asked him, "When is she coming back?"

"Tomorrow," his father replied.

That set Carlos off on a crying spree. "I want ma, I want ma."

His father tried to pacify him but could not. He carried him for a walk around the yard, something he often did, but Carlos was still not satisfied.

"I want ma, I want ma."

In desperation, his father took him to his mother's home. She loved her grandson Carlos and tried to calm him down, but he would not stop crying. After two days without his mother, Carlos adjusted to his father and stopped crying. His father treated him kindly and gave him everything he asked for in order to keep him quiet.

The days went by quickly, and one afternoon his mother appeared in the house. He was very happy to see his mother and ran to her, jumping and laughing. Suddenly, he stood up and saw something strange. His mother had a little person in her hands. She could not lift Carlos in her hands as usual, so he stood up, watching the strange little person. She was his sister, but up to this time, Carlos had only played with toys at home, so he thought his little sister was a toy.

All of a sudden, the little person began to scream, and the sound caused Carlos to cry. His mother tried to pacify both, but Carlos would not stop crying until he was in the arms of his mother. He continued to be curious about that little person who came with his mother.

Finally, he asked her, pointing to the baby, "Where did you get it from?"

"It is her," said his mother. "She is your sister."

"Where she came from?" Carlos asked his mom, who pondered what to tell him. She finally answered, "She came out of my belly."

Carlos's next question was, "Where did she come through?"

"Under my arm," his mother told him.

Carlos did not believe her, and he did not understand her reply until he learned about the reproductive system. He thought his sister was a toy and tried to play with her as he played with his other toys. His mother quickly taught him how to relate to his sister, and he soon learned the difference between his sister and his toys through the warnings and the taps on his hands from his mother.

One day, when his sister was a few months old, Carlos noticed that his mother was not watching him, so he quickly grabbed his sister by her two feet and began swinging her around. His mother rushed to the rescue, but his sister fell to the floor before she could rescue her. She laid still on the floor, unconscious.

His mother was angry, frightened, and frustrated. Suddenly, she thought about something she had read about the use of water to help to regain consciousness. She drenched the little girl with several gallons of water until she showed signs of life and began to cry. Carlos did not remember the incident, but he imagined his tender hide paid for it.

Sibling rivalry began to draw attention from his mother and father. Sometimes, Carlos would protect his sister; other times, he would fight her if she touched his toys. Despite all that, they grew to love each other. They would share their sugar cakes, peppermint candies, bread, cakes, fruits, and anything they were given as gifts. Those relationships are still alive today.

The first five years of Carlos's life were sheltered because his mother guarded him closely and monitored everything he did—even if she was absent when he did something she disliked. What she did not do, his father did when he was not traveling on the sea or attending the small family farm on the steep slopes of James Young Hillside. He was a real watchdog, just like Carlos's mother. One day, Carlos's mother went to visit a friend and left him in the care of his father. While Carlos was playing quietly in the yard, his father walked over to his mother's house a few yards away to chat with her. He took up a position where he could keep an eye on Carlos while he chatted with his mother. After a while, Carlos stopped playing. He thought about something. His mother had a special kind of sugar they called "new sugar," and Carlos loved it.

Why not try to get some of that sugar? a little voice whispered in his ears.

Good thought. So he ran into the house, picked up the jar with the sugar, and began to open it. The jar was closed tightly to prevent ants from getting into the sugar, so Carlos had a hard time trying to get it open. While Carlos struggled, his father appeared at the door and shouted, "I know what you are doing."

Carlos was so frightened that all he could do was to hand over the jar to his father and run away, happy that he was not punished. His father reported the incident to his mother on her return home, and both laughed at his tricks. Carlos heard them talking and laughing, so he felt good that he had escaped punishment—at least, so he thought. Just before going to bed in the evening, before reciting his prayers, he had to face his judge: Mother.

"What did I tell you about meddling with something that does not belong to you?" she asked Carlos.

He was too nervous and frightened to answer immediately, and she waited patiently. Finally, he grumbled, "Do not interfere with it."

"Whose sugar was it that you meddled with today?"

Again, he mumbled, "Yours."

"Listen to me," she said. "The Lord said, 'You shall not steal.' Remember that, and if you are caught again, I will tan your hide."

She loved to "tan your hide," so Carlos tried hard to keep in her good books but failed many times. She never spared the rod. She reminded him in this disciplinary act that he had stepped outside the moral code of the family and the community and, in so doing, displeased the power that controlled their lives. That power came from God. In other words, she told Carlos, he should measure his life by God's standards.

• • •

Carlos would sit and watch his mother weave straw like lightning and knit crochet without watching her fingers. He wondered how on earth she could do these things so fast and so neat. Out of curiosity, he tried to weave straw in his own random fashion without understanding the process. Because he showed such keen interest despite his trials and errors, she taught him how to weave straw. Locally, the people refer to the process as "plaiting teyer." The straw was obtained from the fronds of the Teyer Palm, *coccothrinax argentea (phoenicaceae)* locally called White Teyer and the Silver-Thatch Palm, *thrinax argentea (palmae)* locally called Broom Teyer. He began plaiting five strands, then seven strands, and finally graduated to eleven strands. Again, the local people referred to the strands as splits because they would split a frond of teyer into small strips. Carlos could plait five split, seven split, and eleven splits. That is the way the people spoke about weaving straw. His mother approved his achievements with joy because she saw in him a helper. She was so elated that she told him he plaited eleven splits better than her. That compliment sent his head in the clouds, and he considered himself an accomplished craftsman.

In order to satisfy his ego, he challenged his mother to a competition to see who could plait the most straw in a given period. He was too ambitious, a weakness that can be found in many people. After being defeated a few times, he learned to do his best and not to measure his life by other people's accomplishments. This lesson of doing his best at whatever he was doing was firmly engraved in his mind and heart. It was reinforced through cleaning the yard, cleaning the house, cleaning fish, washing dishes, and when he grew older, washing his home clothes. If the finished product was substandard, he had to repeat the process until it met with his mother's approval. He learned to come straight, not to cut corners, not to take shortcuts, or to try to fool his mother in anything she set him to do. He could not win an argument with his mother, and he concluded that she was the smartest woman in the world. He cherished and enjoyed all the lessons he learned from her.

She trained him to be a good listener through her storytelling sessions. She always told him, "Listen twice as much speak," but warned him never to eavesdrop on other people's conversations. She knew as many stories as possible, including Aesop's Fables and Hans Christian Andersen's fairytales, and all those jumbie stories, treasure stories, land stories, sailors' stories, and stories about people who once lived in the community. Many of those stories have faded from the collective memory of the community because the oral tradition of earlier days is no longer a popular form of communication. In addition to those stories, his mother loved to talk about the struggles of poor people to make two ends meet. Her stories were always well-received, but sometimes after a hair-raising jumbie story, Carlos was too afraid to go to bed.

As mentioned earlier, Carlos was the oldest child in the family, and that meant he would be called upon to perform more domestic chores than any of the other children. Sometimes he had to wake up early in the morning, as early as four o'clock, to help his father and grandfather take care of the cows. This was a feature of the lives of most boys who helped their parents in an agrarian economy. He learned how to milk cows. Sometimes the cows were tethered near the house during the night, and on those occasions, he did not have far to go. Other nights, the cows were tethered or penned on the farm. That meant he would have to walk about two miles to milk the cows. After collecting the milk, he would take it to his mother or grandmother, depending on which cows it came from. It was not very easy to compete with the calves for the milk, but he learned the art and skills rather quickly.

On those mornings when he milked the cows on the farm, he would keep company with a schoolmate nicknamed "Penn," who attended cows on an adjoining farm. Sometimes they shared milk when one of them was delinquent and did not attend to the cows as he should. On one such occasion, Carlos failed to put the cows in the pen, and the following morning the calves had sucked most of the milk from the cows. The little milk he got was less than usual, and Penn was not around that morning to help with some additional milk. Penn's uncle attended to their cows on this occasion.

Carlos thought of a plan to add water to the milk. A voice whispered to him, "Yes, that is the answer."

He added water to the milk. When he caught himself, he had added too much water and made the milk too thin. When he delivered the milk to his grandmother, she looked at it and asked him, "Why is this milk looking so blue?"

He replied, "It was the first milk," which was always thinner than the last milk from the cow.

"First or last," she said, "something is not right with this milk."

Carlos's little heart was pumping at a terrific rate as he pondered what would happen next. If his mother got hold of the story, he would not escape punishment because she was going to investigate like a lawyer until she got the truth. He knew he would not escape punishment for that kind of behavior. The next day, his grandmother looked at the milk and made her comparison with the previous day's milk, which could not "boil up" because it had too much water. She rebuked Carlos for diluting the milk with water. He stood speechless as she reminded him that no one will trust a thief, a liar, or a deceiver. She rubbed her disappointment in him. That day, he repented relentlessly, but guilt ruined his whole day.

Why would he be dishonest with someone who loved him and cared for him? He thought over and over.

Such opportunities for self-examination enabled Carlos to pay special attention to his weaknesses and to search for the right paths that would help him to strengthen those weaknesses. It was not easy for him because he often felt like he was the rope in a tug-o-war, and the forces at the end of the rope were always pulling him in one direction or another. Sometimes, the force was against his will; other times, he felt good on the inside, which signaled to him that he was doing the right thing. The guilt that invaded his consciousness whenever he yielded to the wrong force would remind him that he had violated the moral code that existed in the enclave. His view of life was, "Your feelings are the best guide for right and wrong." Each person has an inner self, a divine self, given by God, and the challenge in life was to let life be your guide. That inner self was not nourished by external success, accolades, honors, or rewards. It gets its strength from a transcendent source. That is why his mother always judged his actions by what the Bible says about the act that may have caused him to step outside the moral boundaries accepted by the community. He began to believe that this inner self was guiding him to his purpose in life. He was thankful that his grandmother did not complain about him to his mother. Double punishment would have been too much.

• • •

We learned earlier that his father and grandfather were fishermen. It was a new experience for him when he made his first trip to the fishing grounds. On that occasion, he was just an observer, bailing water from the bilge of the boat, moving a rope or oar, or any other assigned task. He was curious about the way the men pulled the fish traps from the seabed, landed them in the boat, and took out all the fish through a little trap door, baited the traps with roasted conchs, crabs, or lobsters, and sank them to the seabed again until the next fishing day.

At age six, Carlos met a senior citizen walking to her home, carrying three bundles, one in each hand and the third settled on a cotta on her head. He remembered a story he was told at school titled, "Trouble Made the Monkey Eat Pepper." In the story, an elderly woman was carrying a jar filled with honey when she stubbed her toe, and the jar fell to the ground, spilling the honey. He thought about this woman stubbing her toe and the bundle on her head falling to the ground. She would not be able to hold it because both of her hands were filled. He offered to assist her with one of her bundles, and she gladly accepted. He had to slow his pace to that of the elderly woman. He was not worried because he would have a good reason to give his mother if she rebuked him for idling on the errand.

When they reached the woman's home, he helped her put her bundles inside her door and set off on his errand. She shouted to him, beckoning him to come to her. He ran to her, wondering what the matter was. She stretched forth her hand and placed it on his head, repeating these words, "I do not have a piece of bread I can give you, neither do I have a cent I can give you, but the Lord will bless you."

Carlos felt as if his heart had fallen to the ground. He stood for a few seconds, touched by the woman's actions, then thanked her and ran off. That experience has motivated him throughout his life to be kind to other people, especially senior citizens.

• • •

His mother taught him some culinary skills very early in life, and as he grew older, those skills served him and his family very well. He did not like cleaning fish for her because her standard of completion was very high. She would insist that he clean the belly of the fish with lime until it was white. Today, he expects the same standard from other people and examines fish on his dish before eating it. His mother applied the same standard of cleanliness in the preparation of mutton, beef, pork, and poultry. Sometimes, he argued that she was washing away the strength of the meat. Today, Carlos marvels at chefs who take meat from the grocery wrap and put it directly into the pot. He is very meticulous about eating commercially prepared food.

• • •

Carlos learned some values from his father and mother, which helped him to overcome some dark forces in the community as well as some that were hidden in the recesses of his mind and heart. One of the values he learned early in life was to be punctual. Here are three of the many proverbs his parents recited to him weekly:

1. Time and tide wait for no man.
2. Early bird catches the worm.
3. Strike the iron while it is hot.

Sometimes he got tired of hearing these pronouncements, but he never forgot them. He had to practice them in his daily chores at home. His mother would punish him fiercely for loitering when she sent him on an errand, especially if she found out that he was playing with other children.

When he entered elementary school, he experienced similar behavior. The headmaster would punish students for arriving at school late. Classes began at 9 a.m., and any student who arrived after that time merited punishment. There was no grace period and no negotiation with the student. That behavior was like the behavior at home. He was trapped between these two centers of control over his life, and each one responded in a similar way to punctuality. Another school activity that troubled Carlos was singing a song at the beginning of the school day. The song repeated the same message. It went like this:

> *To be in good time is a necessary rule,*
> *And none should be found,*
> *Coming past the hour to school.*

Oh! How he hated that song, but he had no choice. He had to internalize these lessons so that they could become part of his life. It was part of the process of preparing him for his purpose in life. He was not aware of it at this stage, but it would be revealed to him in the future.

• • •

The value of punctuality was important in his fishing experiences with his father and grandfather. They set their fish traps among the corals to a depth of thirty fathoms. They fastened a rope to the trap, and at the other end, they tied a floating buoy. Then they sank the trap onto the seabed. The buoy would remain as a marker for the trap. In those days, the fishermen did not use rope made from yarn or nylon thread. They cut the running branches of a creeper they called withes. They wove four or five of them together and fastened them with knots at intervals. That guard, as it was called, was hard and tough, so one could imagine the toll on the hands of the fisherman.

After pulling those traps for a long period, Carlos's palms became so tough that he did not feel the roughness of the guard. Sometimes, when the fishermen set the traps, they took identifying landmarks. The more sophisticated fishermen took coordinates with a compass. Carlos was well-trained in this method of fishing and was fascinated by it.

Here, again, he came across the importance of punctuality. The ocean currents among the islands flowed fast at certain times of the day. They are so strong, they sunk the buoys beneath the flowing current. The currents flowed in two directions every twelve hours. When the flow of current changes direction, it flows slowly, the buoys could surface, and the fishermen can harvest the fish. If they missed this window, when the current is flowing slowly and is weak, they would have to wait another twelve hours before they could pull their fish traps.

> *These experiences had a profound influence on his life in determining the kind of adult he would become. He learned to appreciate the peaceful and stormy sunrises and sunsets, the morning, evening, and night rainbows. There was a jingle about the rainbow that people recited whenever they saw one. It goes like this:*

Rainbow in the morning sailors take warning.
Rainbow in the evening weather is deceiving,
Rainbow in the night is the sailor's delight.

Carlos also became a lover of the varying shades of blue in the sea and the azure sky with white clouds floating in the air. He was afraid of the moving waterspout, which was a tornado over the sea. He admired a catch of fish surfacing in a trap from the deep seabed. Among the catch were the trigger fish, angelfish, grouper, snapper, and several other species. The depth below the waves always triggered his imagination, and sometimes he wished he could dive to the bottom of the sea and explore life beneath the waves.

Another observation Carlos reflected on was the tug-of-war between the boat and the ocean current when they were traveling in opposite directions. It was even more noticeable when his father and grandfather had to row a boat for several miles in order to harvest a catch of fish. He recalled a particular channel between Great Camanoe island and Little Camanoe island, where the current flowed very strong, so strong that sailors called the little promontory, "Pull-and-be-Dammed-Point."

Carlos loved to gaze at the sky as he lay on a flat rock with no one to disturb him. He would spend hours reflecting on the daily journey of the sun. The psalmist in Psalm 19 captures that journey eloquently, and John Phillips in his book, *Exploring the Psalms*, expressed the psalmist response as follows:

> *The psalmist watched the sun. He knew where on the horizon the sun entered its tent at night, just where it would emerge next day. He had watched it dissolved the darkness, chase the shadows from the hills and fill the earth with light. He had watched it sink in fiery splendour to its nighttime rest. He had pondered its coming, its career, its character. The sun spoke to all men everywhere without uttering a single word in the language of men.*

Carlos also loved to watch the stars at night and rehearse the stories that he heard about them from his grandparents, parents, and other senior citizens in the community. He absorbed, night after night, the stories that the stars told him through their silent testimonies. He pondered the following nursery rhyme about the stars, which he learned in school:

Twinkle, twinkle, little star
How I wonder what you are!
Up above the world so high
Like a diamond in the sky,
Twinkle, twinkle, little star
How I wonder what you are!

He remembered a poem which expressed the poet's wonder of the skies:

Gaze on the arch above
The glittering vault admire,
Who taught those orbs to move?
Who lit their ceaseless fire?
Who guides the moon and the sun
in silence through the skies?
Who bids the dawning sun
in strength and beauty rise?

Carlos believed the answer to all these questions was the Omnipotent, eternal God who would help him to find his purpose in life.

• • •

The following activity may sound strange to the modern reader who turns on a tap and water flows. The people in the enclave got most of their water from wells. The mineral content of the water differed from well to well. A well supplied from an underground spring with a high mineral content produced water for domestic purposes other than drinking and laundering. The water from springs with low mineral content would be used for drinking, cooking, and laundering. Each household collected water from both types of wells and stored it in special containers outside the house.

During periods of drought, the wells produced less water, and according to the number of persons taking water from a well, it would run dry. The spring produced water slowly, so everyone would have to wait, sometimes for several hours, before they could get water. During those periods, everyone waited until the well was replenished. This was a kind of water rationing that enabled everyone to get some water. Carlos was caught in situations like this many times. Sometimes he arrived at the well too late; other times, although he arrived on time, the large crowd would push him to the back of the line, and his waiting period would be extended.

• • •

Before ending this chapter, let me tell you about his first visit to the capital, Road Town, on a Saturday. He was all excited when his mother told him on the previous Thursday that she would be taking him to Road Town. He could hardly sleep the night before the visit. He stayed awake thinking about this new adventure. Before dawn, he was up and around, waiting for instructions from his mother. He completed all his assigned tasks in record time and was ready to head for the Red Bay jetty. As he walked alongside his mother to the jetty, his little heart was thumping against his chest with anxiety. He felt like a little prince. Once inside the ferry, he sat and watched the adults moving around, selecting their seats, and securing their belongings. The ferry horn signaled its departure, and Carlos was off on an excursion.

The ride on the ferry was frightening as the boat rolled with the waves. The wind was strong, and the waves were high. As they journeyed over the waves, the passengers became concerned, if not frightened. A few of them were thrown from their seats while others became sick. The crew was very polite and attended to the sick passengers until they recovered.

When the ferry was berthed at the Road Town jetty, everyone was relieved and disembarked joyfully and hastily because they only had about five hours to do their business. The women who carried straw hats and bags to sell hurried to their stalls, where some customers were waiting for them. The sales took place in the marketplace, which was very busy on Saturday—market day. People from all areas of the British Virgin Islands went to Road Town on market day to buy food supplies, household appliances, building materials, and materials for the fishermen's traps. Fish was one of the fastest-selling commodities, but locally butchered beef, mutton, and pork were also in great demand. All kinds of agricultural produce would be on sale, sometimes more than the people needed. Other people traveled to Road Town to visit the doctor. It was the most convenient time for people to seek medical attention as there was no vehicular transportation. A few people traveled to visit relatives and friends, and that was also an occasion to exchange gifts.

Carlos's mother introduced him to her friends who had only heard about him. They were delighted to meet him, and each one described him in one sentence. One description offended him and remained with him. One of his mother's friends said about, "He is going to be a proud man. See how he is standing?" Carlos had already learned that being proud is culturally unacceptable, and that made her comment unpleasant. He decided quietly that he was going to prove to her that she was wrong. Many years passed, and he interacted with her on many occasions, especially when his mother sent him to carry fish for her. She was always kind and friendly, but Carlos remembered her first comment on him.

One day, she told him in the presence of some of her children that he was her son and they were his brothers and sisters. He was overwhelmed by that statement and the reception that he was given by her children. Carlos was conscious of the attitude of the people in the community who seemed to have a mission to define who a person is or predict a person's character. He recalled hearing many expressions that reflected that attitude.

A few of them are:

"He looks like his father."

"He walks like his great grandfather."

"He speaks like a Yankee."

"He writes like a girl."

"He thinks she is better than everybody else."

"He is a polite fellow."

"He is going to be a sailor like his grandfather."

"He can't be any better because his parents live in the bush."

"He ain't going to learn anything because he is absent from school too often."

"You're stupid, just like your father."

"He can't make anything."

"His mind is bigger than his body."

Whenever anyone made any comment on his life, he would get upset for a short while because he was prepared to "paddle his own canoe." He was determined to follow a path similar to what E. E. Cummings described in the following passage:

To be nobody but yourself in a world which is doing its best, night and day, to make you everybody else, means to fight the hardest battle which any human being can fight, and never stop fighting.

Carlos's aim was to get a clearer understanding of who he was born to be because he was convinced that everything else would fall into place. His belief was based on Jesus's words in the Gospel According to Matthew, Chapter 6, Verse 23: "Seek ye first the Kingdom of God and all these things would be added to you." He wanted to identify his core being that purpose for which he was created, his strengths in life, his values, and his passions. He was encouraged by these words by George Bernard Shaw:

This is the true joy in life, the being used for a purpose, recognized by yourself as a mighty one.

His mother took him to visit other friends who were not in the marketplace. The visits were short because she was a vendor of straw products, and she had to attend to her business. One of the things Carlos observed, and it remained with him, was the vendors of straw products assisted one another with sales. They seemed to take turns to do other business while the other vendors sold their products. This cooperative behavior appealed to Carlos and was a reassurance to him that he wanted to serve people, to help people wherever and whenever he had the opportunity to do so.

He remembered a very unusual experience on that day. His mother took him to meet his paternal grandmother's cousin and left him with her while she did some chores. He sat quietly in the living room, looking at the pictures on the wall. In the room was the woman's only daughter, an adult who had a grave speech impediment and kept chewing and grumbling all the time. Every now and then, she pointed to Carlos as if to ask him why he was there. He could not understand what she was saying, and he felt very uncomfortable in her presence. Sometimes he was fearful when she made various gestures that he could not understand. He felt like this was going to ruin his day. After having so much fun meeting other people, he felt like a captive.

Suddenly, the thought came to him that she needed help. He was unable to help her, but he began to empathize with her. He remembered the stories of Jesus healing people and helping them out of their distress. He thought that somebody should help her. Poor woman! He left, hoping that he would hear something good happened to her.

It was nearing the time to embark on the ferry to return home. Carlos remembered his sister and brother at home and wanted to carry something for them. This was an early expression of the thoughts that occupied his mind from day to day. He observed how his mother cared for other people. He was especially intrigued by the time she devoted to needy people who would stop at her house to ask for alms. It seemed that she believed it was her duty to treat them well. They must have appreciated it because they seemed to be comfortable making those visits because they felt at home.

He had a little money, which he got from his mother and two of his uncles, whom he met for the first time. Those uncles were fishermen, and they lived on Salt Island and Peter Island, just across Drakes Channel from where she lived. He bought some sugar-babies (a special type of candy) and lollipops for them. He had to hide the candies because his mother forbade him from eating any candies. When she discovered what he had done, she scolded him for his disobedience, but he did not mind because the joy of having something special for his siblings overwhelmed her scolding. He thought what he was doing for his brothers and sisters was more important than eating the forbidden candies.

Departure time was fast approaching. Everyone was taking her packages to the ferry. The traffic was heavy because the captain was a punctual man, and he did not wait for anyone. Soon the captain arrived, smiling, and the pace of embarking on the ferry increased. Everyone had to be onboard when the clock struck the hour for departure. Luckily, everyone was safe onboard, and the journey home began. The women shared jokes and laughed at some of the things they experienced. The sea was smooth and friendly, making the ride home more comfortable. The arrival at Red Bay was another busy session. People who expected packages were there to receive them. The passengers moved around frantically, looking for their unlabeled belongings. The hustle and bustle soon died down, the jetty was empty, the ferry had departed, and everyone headed home. This was a day to remember, and he never forgot it.

Those activities were the prelude to a challenging life that lay ahead. Although these experiences alluded to difficult times in life, he found them useful in helping to mold his character. They taught him respect for other people, patience when pressed by undesirable forces, a good work ethic, and to take every opportunity to help other people, especially those who were less fortunate.

CHAPTER THREE
Boyhood Adventures

*"Boyhood is a most complex and incomprehensible thing.
Even when one has been through it, one does
not understand what it was. A man can never quite
understand a boy, even when he has been a boy."*
— **Gilbert K. Chesterton**

Carlos introduced his three close friends earlier, but he will tell you more about them in this chapter. Their names were Brent, King, and Will. All four moved around like quads, but the oldest member was two years older than the youngest member. Shortly after they formed the group, Carlos discovered that there some fundamental differences between his friends' collective beliefs and behaviors and his.

He listened attentively to the public discourses within the enclave and in the wider community. He remembered that his mother had told him on many occasions that it is always more difficult to swim upstream than to swim with the current. She meant for him to understand that it is always easier to follow the crowd than to follow your own decisions. He believed it was important for him to understand the people in his neighborhood and the environment in which he lived. He loved the quotation by Socrates, "know thyself," and he took it as his guiding star. His friends were not interested in these issues, and whenever he attempted to share his views with them, they dismissed him.

Brent would say, "One should cross a bridge when you reached it and should not plan how to cross it in advance."

King and Will would echo, "Carlos, you are always planning, and your plans do not come through."

Carlos would simply say, "every man to his own order."

This was one of the differences between Carlos and his friends. He loved his friends but hated their carefree attitude to life and their habits of smoking cigarettes and drinking alcoholic drinks.

One afternoon after school, all four of them were relaxing when Brent suddenly took some cigarettes from his pocket and began to share them around.

"Take one, Carlos," he said, handing him a cigarette.

"I do not smoke cigarettes," replied Carlos.

King joined the conversation. "Just give it a try, Carlos," he said.

"I do not have to try it to know that I do not like it," Carlos said. "The smell is enough and, furthermore, I do not have any chimney in my head."

Will burst a laugh and shouted, "What a coward!"

"If that is being a coward, then so be it," Carlos responded in a commanding tone.

He refused to bow to his friends, who knew that they could not push him too far without serious consequences. They depended on Carlos to help them with their school assignments.

Carlos thought seriously about their perceptions of life. He even wondered if they could be right, and he was on the wrong side. Come what may, he dismissed the idea and followed his own passion.

Another difference between Carlos and his friends was Carlos tended to be more introverted while his friends were all extroverted. Carlos was not always introverted, but when he was with his friends, he displayed this characteristic. He seemed to operate from extremes, strongly hating something and strongly liking other things. He hated the middle ground because it represented mediocrity in his mind, a characteristic he just could not tolerate. He believed in striving for excellence. He had to learn that the world was not black and white, and there was a range of possibilities when looking at a situation. He always wanted to satisfy himself that he had done his best when faced with any problem. His aim to be always armed with the relevant knowledge and skills was good, but he had to understand that sometimes one would have to search for them before they could be applied to a situation.

His mother said to him many times, "Mother may have, Father may have, but blessed is the child who has his own."

She taught him how to think independently, never to depend on anyone, and to use his brain for himself.

Carlos also differed from his three friends in his sense of security. He learned very early to put his faith in God, who could guard him against all evil and guide him on the right path in life. His parents spent a lot of time explaining the importance of relying on God for help. They taught him passages of scripture like the 23rd Psalm: "The Lord is my shepherd; I shall not want."

His friends had their sense of security grounded in the power and authority, which their fathers exhibited in the enclave. Their parents taunted other residents with their economic power, their strong hold on real estate, as well as "clandestine extrasensory powers." He was never comfortable in the presence of his friends when they touted the ability of their parents to take care of them. His friends thought it was a wonderful feeling to be able to rely on their parents for protection even when they were wrong. Carlos strongly believed in being independent and free to make his own decisions and face the consequences of those decisions.

One moonlight night, he and his friends, plus a few other boys from the community, were playing games. Suddenly, an unusually shaped elderly man walked toward his home, and the boys began to tease him. Carlos did not join in that behavior because his mother had instructed him to respect elderly people and help them if they needed it.

Carlos was wearing a hat and, out of nowhere, a gust of wind came and blew his hat at the feet of the elderly man. The man stood up, stooped down, picked up the hat, and folded it in his arms. Carlos could not go home without his hat, for he would have to account to his mother for it. He had to get that hat, but none of his friends were willing to assist him in retrieving it.

The old man stood up, hugged the hat snuggly in his arms, and said, "I am going to repay the owner of this hat."

They all ran home, leaving Carols to recover his hat. He approached the elderly man and asked him for it. While he was giving the hat to Carlos with his left hand, the elderly man slapped him on his jaw with his right hand and uttered these words, "Take that for teasing an old man."

Carlos's anger increased beyond control; he took up a stone and was about to strike the old man when a voice suddenly said to him, "You are known by the company you keep, so drop that stone."

That had to be his mother's voice repeating one of her famous quotations to him. He aborted his attack reluctantly and accepted his fate. He kept in mind a quotation his mother told him many times, "If you lie down with dogs, you will catch their flees."

He could not tell his mother what had happened, but when he reached home, she discerned something was not right and tried unsuccessfully to find out what it was.

After that incident, Carlos was very careful when he was in the company of his friends. His interactions with them were very controlled and subdued. They tried to mend the broken relationship, but Carlos's trust in them was diminished after that experience. That encounter taught him to be aware of the actions of other people, to better respect elderly people, and to develop a keener sense of what was true friendship. That experience was a turning point in Carlos's boyhood relationships with his friends.

His parents, especially his mother, were not very comfortable with his membership in the group and warned and counseled him very often about the activities the group was known to be engaged in inside the enclave. If the group happened to perform an act that offended some of the inhabitants of the enclave, the news spread very quickly, and, once his parents heard it, he had to appear before them to give an account of his part in the act. He would have to tell them the truth because they would investigate the incident behind his back. Carlos was always concerned about the ease with which his parents got information about his behavior. It seemed that people were always watching him and reporting to his parents what they saw him doing. He hated that characteristic of the people in the enclave and the community. They were always prying into the affairs of other people. In Carlos's case, they did it because they knew his parents would listen to them. The following episode is a typical example.

One afternoon, Carlos's mother sent him to the bakery to purchase bread. He met two of his friends—King and Will. They were also running errands for their parents. King rejoiced when he saw Carlos and shouted, "Let's play a game of marbles."

Carlos was reluctant, but Will talked him into playing the game.

"Just a short game, Carlos, and then we will run off on our errands."

One game ended, a second game ended, and in the middle of the third game, a nosy, inquisitive woman passed them and said, "Quit playing marbles and go on your parents' business."

She recognized Carlos and went directly to his home and reported that she had passed him, along with two other boys, playing marbles. The woman spoke loudly, and one of the neighbors who loved Carlos called him on his way home and warned him that a woman had lodged a complaint about him. He used to run errands for this woman because she did not have any children, and she always looked out for him. Carlos asked for a description of the woman, and he realized it was that same nosy woman who met them on the road.

When he reached home, his mother scolded him for playing along the road with his friends. He tried to find out who had made the complaint, but his mother refused to tell him. She gently reminded him that somebody was always watching him, so he ought to be upright and careful. Carlos did not disclose to his mother that he knew who the informant was. After that incident, he kept an eye on that nosy woman whenever he met her. He hated to greet her, but if he did not do it, she would complain about him to his mother, and she would punish him for violating the moral code of behavior that the family upheld.

Carlos became known as a reliable person in the enclave. Many senior citizens would ask him to do them favors, and he met their requests faithfully. When he met his friends, he would join them in various activities before completing the mission he was currently carrying out.

He loved to play with matches that he could strike on any hard surface and ignite. In the community, people called those matches "knockabout matches." The village shops sold them two for one cent or three for two cents. One day, he had two cents and bought three matches. He looked around for some dry grass to set ablaze for pleasure. He saw the ideal spot, scratched a match, and threw it in the grass. It was a large field of dry grass, for rain had not fallen for several months, and it was dry all around. The grass caught fire, and the blaze raced over the field with terrific speed. The fire was out of control. Carlos became confused and frightened and took off running, hoping that no one would see him. His mother had told him that unseen eyes were always watching him, but he had forgotten that.

Other eyes were also watching him on this occasion, for as soon as he began to run, a woman shouted with a loud voice, "You little vagabond, I am going to complain you to your mother."

The fire attracted onlookers, but it died down quickly. That woman announced to everybody she met that Carlos was playing with matches and started the fire. Everyone looked at him in disappointment because he was such a polite and friendly fellow. They warned him to stop playing with matches. His mother was angry and disappointed, and so was the punishment she administered. That was the end of Carlos's habit of playing with matches.

When his friends heard the outcry about what Carlos had done, they looked for him to give him support, but they could not find him. His mother had isolated him for twelve hours, and he was not allowed to speak to anyone during that time. He had to kneel and hold a book in his right hand in the air for one hour and then change it to his left hand for another hour. Carlos kept his eyes on her because she seemed to have had eyes in the back of her head. Whenever he thought that she was attending to something, he would take down his hand. At the slightest movement of her body, he would put his hand in the air. The time in punishment was spent playing that little game.

After he had served his time in punishment, he found his friends. Brent reminded him that he had warned him about playing with matches, but he would not listen. King supported Brent and reinforced their warning. By that time, Carlos had already decided that he was finished with that habit. He thanked his friends for their encouragement, and they all laughed at the incident.

In addition to those three friends, Carlos also kept secrets for two aunts. His mother's youngest sister lived in the home with him for a few years, and his father's youngest sister by adoption lived with his grandmother. Both young women were about the same age, and each of them agreed to keep Carlos's secrets, and he agreed to keep theirs. Each of these young women had their secret boyfriend, and Carlos knew about the relationships. When they had to attend evening functions, he was always selected to be their chaperone. He was very glad for those opportunities to play with his friends. On these occasions, the young women would meet their boyfriends. The stories of these meetings were never rehearsed because Carlos was a trusted confidante, and his aunts were always kind to him. He learned to be honest with people as he grew older. This was one of the lessons his mother taught him very early in life. His students soon discovered that they could trust him, and they shared their problems with him confidentially. They believed that he would help them during challenging times, and they were never disappointed. Many of them became lifelong friends.

• • •

He had to perform specific tasks for the family. These included gathering dry wood, collecting water from wells, plaiting straw, burning charcoal, laundering for the household, cooking, fishing, and sailing boats to sell produce. Collecting dry wood for the oven and the fireplace was a daily chore. He usually collected the wood in the morning before going off to school. Sometimes he collected it after the school day. Meals were usually prepared over a charcoal fire, but sometimes firewood was used. Carlos loved to burn a coal pit. The wood was collected and stored by the coalpit bed until there was enough wood to build the coalpit. He then placed the wood neatly on the prepared bed in the pit. The wood would then be covered with a thick layer of green branches, mainly mangrove, and then buried under a thick layer of earth. A small opening was made for lighting the pit, and a few openings at the opposite end allowed the gases to escape as the heat turned the wood into charcoal.

Sometimes he would collect wood with his three friends. On such occasions, they competed to collect the largest quantity of wood that one could carry comfortably. One time, Carlos's bundle of wood was too heavy for him to carry. This he discovered when they ready to head home. His friends began to laugh at him and went home, leaving him behind to make the adjustments to his bundle of wood. By the time he got through his adjustments, his friends were nowhere to be seen. He was very disappointed by the actions of his friends and vowed not to speak to them for the day.

That morning, he was late to arrive at school and was punished, as was the custom. His friends escaped punishment because they made it to school on time. He kept away from them for some time because he knew that he would get them in the palm of his hands. Within a few days, they needed his assistance with their assignments. King could not solve his math problems. He repented for his part in the plot on the morning when they left him to adjust his bundle of wood. He asked for forgiveness and begged for help with his assignments. Before Carlos agreed to help King, he asked him to kneel before him with his hands in the air while Carlos counted from one to fifty. King obeyed without resistance. Carlos felt sorry for punishing his friend. However, he helped him with his work and amended their friendship.

Will also repented and made his peace with Carlos, but Brent laughed at their cowardice. He finally conceded when he had to prepare for a class test, and he was experiencing some difficulties.

"Carlos," he said, "let us make up, man. I won't encourage those boys to desert you again."

"I need some time to think about it," Carlos replied.

"Come on, man, I will pay you twenty-five cents to help me," Brent said.

"That sounds good, but you will have to pay me before I work," Carlos replied.

Brent, with tears in his eyes, pleaded, "Lord, Carlos, I don't have the money now, but I expect a job soon, and I will pay you when I finish the job."

Carlos was not interested in payment for helping Brent but agreed with his proposal in order to prove his integrity. Carlos helped him, he passed the test, he paid the money, which Carlos returned, and their friendship was restored.

Carlos had already begun to understand that the best values in life are not grounded in material things. He did not want their friendship to be tied to what any member of the group could get from other members.

Although Carlos was not the official leader of the pack, he tried to guide the members into activities that all of them could enjoy and help them to grow to be more caring, loving, and kind to one another and others outside the group. Sometimes, he met with stiff resistance from his friends, who would remind him that he did have any authority over them. He never got offended by them and continued to stand firm in his beliefs.

When the group had vacation, they used many of the days to cement their friendship through group activities. Here is a typical example: After breakfast on a summer day, the group assembled on James Young Bay to plan the program for that day.

"King, what are your plans for today?" asked Brent, the leader of the group.

On this day, the boys had decided to have a picnic on Red Rock, an outcrop of red metamorphic rocks in East End harbor. Over the years, the sea had deposited tons of white sand around these rocks and created a small beach. There was just enough land space for a few shade trees, cooking space, water storage, and a catch of fish, which formed part of the picnic's lunch. They secured a boat, food supplies, and fishing gear. The rowing expedition across the harbor was exciting. All the members of the group could row, so they took turns, two at a time.

On arrival at Red Rock, everyone disembarked and took all the belongings to the picnic site. Those who were assigned to fish went on their way. The others were responsible for the management of the site, preparing the grounds and the meals. The site crew gathered firewood for the fireplace, where the cooking would take place. Most of the day was spent in the sea, swimming and playing water games.

As the day wore on, everyone performed the assigned duties as expected, and everyone enjoyed the day. Before the group packed up their belongings to return home, they made a final check to make sure that everything was in order. Each one made sure that the belongings included enough whelks for a family meal. This was provided to prove to the other members of the families that they were not forgotten.

Carlos and his friends also enjoyed picking seasonal fruits and sharing them with their friends and family members inside and outside the enclave. These fruits included tamarinds, genips, guavas, sugar-apples, sea-grapes, and cashews. All these fruit trees were on private properties, and children would have to get permission to pick them. On many occasions, the children would trespass on the properties to reap fruits. Sometimes the owners would ignore them; other times, the owners would rebuke and threaten them if they returned. In many cases, such communication fell on deaf ears because the same children would repeat their pranks.

The children had rules that governed the reaping of fruits, such as tamarinds and guavas. Girls were forbidden from climbing the tamarind trees because the boys believed the tree would bear sour tamarinds if that happened. The boys had to climb the trees pick the fruits, and share them with the girls. That rule was challenged one day when a girl named Anna was caught picking tamarinds. The boys wanted to punish her, but they knew they had no authority to do so, and they would have to face the judgment of the community. The sweet part of the challenge was when Anna took up two stones, one in each hand, and challenged the boys to battle.

"Anyone of you think you bad? Touch me!"

She waited, but no one dared accept her challenge. She walked away, victorious. Women power!

Guavas were another prized fruit for boys and girls as they traveled to and from school and on errands for their parents. Some trees grew along the roadside and were easily accessed. There was a scary story among children that if one ate too many guavas with the seeds, one would become constipated. The vulgar name for this phenomenon was "plug up." One day, the news spread among the children that Jill had eaten too many guavas with seeds, and she was "plug up." Her parents were angry because they had warned her about the danger of eating too many guavas in one sitting. She was overly excited about the juicy yellow fruits that she had discovered on a tree and forgot her parents' admonitions. Luckily, there was a folk doctor who knew how to "unplug" children living near her home. Her parents were able to get relief for her. "Children, obey your parents."

Genips were also very common in the village. When it was genip season, anyone, including girls, could climb the genip trees and reap the fruits. There were some prized genip trees on certain properties and the boys enjoyed climbing the fences to get them. One day, an elderly man went to guard his genip tree, which bore the sweetest genips in the village. While waiting patiently, he fell asleep under the tree. The boys arrived quietly, climbed the tree, picked the genips, descended the tree, and placed a few bunches of the fruits on his chest as he snored in the cool tropical breeze. When he woke up, he was surprised and angry but could do nothing but take the genips and walk home.

Eating these tropical fruits was good entertainment as well as a nutritional benefit to the body. Today the residents in the enclave must purchase these fruits from the supermarket if they are lucky. Even then, they are treated with chemicals for preservation, and that is not good for one's health. The youthful spirit of comradery and unity among boys and girls sitting and enjoying juicy, ripe tropical fruits in the open air, in the shade of a large tree, with the cool tropical breeze rustling through the leaves no longer exists.

• • •

At home, Carlos enjoyed life with his siblings. They did not have access to the types of toys that children have today. They made their own toys. The boys spun tops, which they made from pieces of wood shaped to size with a nail inserted at the narrow end of the top. They made sure that the wood was balanced on all sides as they sanded their tops to a smooth finish. If there was any imbalance, the top would not spin. Carlos and his friends played games like aiming for the bullseye with their tops. One boy would place his top on the ground, and, one by one, the boys would try to split that top with their tops. If the boy failed in destroying his friend's top, the roles were then reversed. The boy who failed in his efforts now placed his top on the ground, and the other players would try to destroy his top. They would take turns putting up the tops to be destroyed.

His siblings and friends also made ukuleles by getting large, empty sardine cans for the sound boxes. Then they inserted a piece of board at one end of each can with markings representing frets. The next stage was to fasten the strings made from strong twine to the sound boxes and the keys at the other end of the boards. They would then tune the instruments and play music. They would select special tins for drums and make drumsticks from branches of trees. They made flutes from the stems of the papaya leaves. When they combined these instruments, they had rudimentary fungi bands.

The boys also made boats sculpted from logs of wood taken from certain trees, mainly the turpentine tree. The shipwrights in the village would assist the boys in sculpting the wood to produce the best boats. These boats were called log boats because they were made from logs of wood. Sailing these boats in the harbor was a pleasant pastime for the boys. They would swim with their boats, or they would follow the boats in a rowboat.

The girls made dolls from pieces of cloth and played with them when they did not have imported dolls. Sometimes, they pretended to be mothers and built dollhouses. On special occasions, a group of boys and a group of girls would merge to form a make-believe family. A girl would be nominated as mother and a boy as father. All the other members of the group were children. Relationships and reactions on these occasions were varied and exciting. At the end of the day, play was meaningful to all of them and kept them together as relatives and friends.

・・・

During all these activities, Carlos was always conscious of that transcendent power that guided him. He was searching for meaning in his life. That consciousness was strengthened when his mother told him that there were unseen eyes watching him every day. His internal self seemed to be connected to that power and provided an understanding of the problems he encountered. That connection provided a calm, reassuring feeling that anchored his life amidst the turbulence in the environment. It was a kind of internal coherence. Somehow, he felt that God would make a way for him and his duty was to keep his heart clean so that God would abide in him.

As a boy, Carlos attended prayer meetings with his grandmother, and the experiences he gained from attending those meetings added another dimension to his belief in God. He loved to attend the meetings and listen to the prayers of the older people. There were musical rhythms to their prayers. They spoke with certainty that their prayers were being heard by someone and they would be answered. Another concept that came to his consciousness as he listened to them praying was the fact that they seemed to be making deposits to a body of prayer that was somewhere stored or recorded on their behalf. Every time they prayed, that store increased. It was like the principal in a bank account. Every deposit made the principal larger. As Carlos listened to the discourses in the community about the power of prayer, he realized that for these people, prayer was their lifeline. Every success by an individual was attributed to the prayers of the family. Conversely, failures, misfortunes, or what they called bad luck were attributed to the lack of sincere prayers by the affected individuals and the close relatives of those individuals.

"I attend those prayer meetings voluntarily," Carlos told his friends when they questioned him about following old people. He invited them to join him many times, but they always shied away from his invitations and laughed at him. Those boys believed in themselves. They believed their success came through their own labor. Carlos never agreed with them on such issues and never got angry with them. He wanted to help them to become better people. Carlos's parents and siblings also never showed any interest in attending those meetings. He would extend invitations from time to time, especially if there were visiting preachers, but they never accepted. He discovered, in a very quiet way, that his father was suspicious that he was using prayer meetings as a cover for more amorous adventures, as was the custom among young men. He discovered this through remarks his father made from time to time. Carlos never responded to his father's comments, so if they were "sprats to catch a whale," he did not fish well.

Carlos loved to attend all-night prayer meetings. These meetings were held in special homes throughout the island—mostly on Friday nights because the following day could be used for rest. A group of young people from his village would travel to another village on a Friday afternoon and spend the night singing, praying, and rejoicing. They would return home on Saturday morning and join in their regular work routine accordingly. The excursion was healthy because all the travel was walking. There were no motorable roads during those years of the early 1950s. While preparing for one of these journeys, Carlos happened to overhear his father's lament to his mother. He was suspicious that Carlos was using the occasions for love affairs. His mother rebuked his father for his suspicious views about her son's behavior. His father was very conservative, while his mother was more liberal in her outlook on life. Carlos never let them know that he was aware of their different evaluations of his behavior. He kept his focus on the goal to discover his purpose in life.

Another day, Carlos was so upset by one of his father's comments that he found Brent and said to him, "Can you imagine that my father is suspicious that I am not attending prayer meetings, but using the occasions for other purposes?"

"But, Carlos, the men tease your father for not having another woman outside his marriage, so why would he suspect you?"

"I do not know. Maybe he hears stories about other boys, and he puts me in that category."

"Maybe," said Brent. "However, everybody knows that you are afraid of girls, so why should he be worried?"

"What did you say, Brent? Afraid of girls! I respect girls. I am not like you who disrespect them."

"Let me tell you, Carlos, I don't respect them; I just use them for what they can do."

"Shame on you, Brent," said Carlos. "I hope you will change your mind before you have daughters."

"I have to run, Carlos; I will see you tomorrow."

Brent's attitude was common in those days. Most young men never considered that lifestyle immoral. Carlos feared for his friends because he believed they were not fair to themselves and other people. They found pleasure in imposing themselves on others, on behaving arrogantly, especially in the presence of their peers, dominating situations by the show of force on the most vulnerable, especially girls. They did not attribute their achievements to anyone other than themselves. He believed in a different set of values, like not following the flow of the dominant traffic and trying to reshape his understanding of his neighbors and enemies by the inspiration he got from God. The prayer meetings were one medium through which he communicated with God.

When there was a revival in the village—that is, a great outpouring of the Holy Spirit—large numbers of people would attend prayer meetings, and many would dedicate their lives to God. The process of dedication was like a cultural rite of passage. The penitents spent long hours kneeling before the altar, sometimes beating the altar with their hands—praying, crying, and pleading, at times—moving their bodies in response to the singing, which continued throughout the process. Some people would say they were under conviction; others would say they were "were licking out their sins." The penitents were expected to stay in that state until their sins were forgiven. Then they could rise and testify to the pardon they had received. Sometimes, according to the way they give their testimonies, the people would doubt them as being sincere and accused them of fake testimonies. This was a challenge for them to prove their faith in God.

Revival time was also fun time for some people. Many attended the meetings only to look on, while others hoped that they would be fortunate to find sexual partners. It was well known that there was always an increase in the population nine months after revival campaigns. Carlos's interest, of course, in attending these meetings enhanced his spiritual strength through prayers, singing, and the preached word. This was part of the spiritual legacy of his grandmother that helped to define his purpose in life. Those prayer meetings no longer exist. They have faded away with the cultural changes that have swept through the territory.

CHAPTER FOUR
School Days

"Criticisms may not be agreeable, but it is necessary. It fulfills the same function as a pain in the human body. It calls attention to the unhealthy state of things."
— **Winston Churchill**

The first five years of Carlos's life were filled with lots of adventure inside the enclave. He was curious to learn about things around him and why people behaved the way they did. Much of his curiosity was centered around the past life of his parents, particularly his mother. He questioned her regularly about her parentage, her siblings, her life on Salt Island, her life in East End, and her life within the enclave. She shared these experiences with him willingly. He was very much interested in the stories of her school days and was even challenged to exceed her accomplishments, which were outstanding for that time.

Every day, he tried to improve his literacy and numeracy skills in preparation for school registration. Sometimes, he felt that the time for registration would never come. At last, the day came for him to be registered in school. He was about to begin a ten-year program of formal education. That morning, Carlos was so excited he could hardly contain himself. He felt proud walking by his mother's side to the school, which was housed in the Methodist Church, the only church in the village at that time to be registered.

It was a place for divine worship on Sunday and on Monday, a schoolhouse and a community center serving the villages of East End, Long Look, Hope Estate, and Brandy Wine Bay. It served as a concert hall for musical performances and drama. The annual Christmas concert by the students was always well-attended by parents and friends. Weddings took place periodically during the school day. During these ceremonies, all instruction was suspended, and the students became "wedding guests." The invited guests occupied the front rows, and the students sat behind them. Everyone had to remain quiet until the ceremony ended and the wedding party had departed. School then continued as usual. Carlos learned later that there was only one minister for eight congregations scattered on four different islands—Tortola, Anegada, Virgin Gorda, and Jost Van Dyke. There were no motorable roads, and he had to walk, ride a horse, or sail across the channels on the Tortola boat or the occasional ferry to minister to his congregations.

In addition to registration, that was Carlos's first day at school. He met new boys and girls as well as some whom he had met before at Sunday School or on the village playgrounds. He was placed in what the school called Junior A, which was like modern-day kindergarten, only the lessons were more formal. He had to train his memory because there was no internet to turn to for information, and there were very few books available for young students like Carlos. He had to write on a slate. It was a slab of shale carved from the earth and prepared for writing. The main disadvantage of the slate was one could not save one's notes for any period besides the time allotted for the lesson.

The new school environment extended his world, so he began to relate to the other students and teachers, and responded to the instruction.

That day, he saw his friends Bert and King, but Will was not ready to enroll in school. These two friends were not in his grade, and he only saw them when they had a break from classes. Carlos spent most of his time that day exploring his new environment. The various voices of teachers as they taught their classes attracted his attention. As he gazed from grade to grade, he realized students were engaged in a wide range of activities. He began to wonder what it would be like when he reached those higher grades.

In the middle of his daydream, his teacher called him to her desk for some important instructions. He could not understand why so many students spoke at the same time. This was prohibited at home. He had to listen when someone was speaking. At the end of his first day, he began to understand his new world. He was not aggressive, but he was bold, pushy, and commanding. Little by little, he gained control over his challenges.

Back home, his little sister was curious to learn what school was like. Before he settled at home, she began her inquiries about school and to challenge Carlos's knowledge. She loved to boast about her knowledge and tried to compete with him, who was less talkative. By the time she entered school, she was challenging him. When she learned a new word or a new idea, she would run to her dad or her mother, telling them about her revelation. They loved that and expected Carlos to behave in a similar way. He had a mind of his own and did not allow her or his parents to force him to behave like her. He decided if they wanted to test his knowledge, they would have to question him, and they did that periodically during the week.

After returning home from his first day at school, he went to visit his grandmother to tell her about school. She was a well-respected woman in the enclave, and he felt proud of her. His grandfather was there when he paid the visit and said to him, "Study hard if you want to get a good job when you grow up." That admonition stayed with Carlos and was one of his motivating goals during school. His grandmother congratulated him and reminded him not to pick her pomegranates. That story of Carlos and his grandmother's pomegranates is an interesting one that he would like to share with you.

His grandmother had a lovely pomegranate tree, which was always laden with fruit of varying sizes and hundreds of bright red pomegranate blossoms. A beauty to behold! The tree bore pomegranates year-round. Some of the fruits were green in color; others were red like blood, and still others were orange in color according to their ages. When you looked at them, your salivary glands woke up and started working at an accelerated rate. Carlos watched his grandmother's pomegranates day after day, longing to get one to eat. His grandmother watched her pomegranates like a thrush, waiting for the day when she thought they were ready for harvest. One day there so many pomegranates that he decided to pick one, hoping that his grandmother would not miss it. He was wrong.

After returning home from Sunday School one sunny afternoon, his grandmother called him to her house, which was close by—all the houses in the enclave were close to one another. He felt happy because he thought she had called him for his usual share of her cooking, which she reserved for him on Sunday. To his surprise, she addressed him.

"Carlos, where is my pomegranate?"

He waited several minutes before he could reply. What was he to say to her? He told a lie, denying that he had picked her pomegranate. She did not believe him. She pronounced a guilty verdict without any further interrogation.

"You picked my pomegranate, and do not do that again without my permission."

She further admonished him that it was wrong to steal from another person. He remembered what his mother had told him when he was caught stealing her sugar. He tried to convince himself that picking his grandmother's pomegranate was not stealing. He cared for the tree, keeping it free from weeds and pruning it without pay. He decided to ignore his grandmother's warning because the temptation to eat some of those pomegranates was too strong. He fell on a plan to tuck some of the branches with a few pomegranates in the middle of the tree in such a way that she would never see them from her guard station—her rocking chair by the door. He monitored those tucked-away pomegranates until they were ripe, and then he had his desire—juicy pomegranates. There was no rebuke because his grandmother never saw them. He felt like a champion because he thought that he was smarter than his grandmother.

Sometime not too long after that episode, he overheard his parents talking about the unseen eyes that were always watching you. A feeling of guilt overwhelmed him because his conscience told him those eyes were watching him as he ate his grandmother's pomegranates without her permission. To make matters worse for him, when his grandmother reaped her pomegranates, she would always save his share. This feeling made him uncomfortable for several days.

Then, one day, he heard a voice asking him, "Why are you stealing from your grandmother, who loves you so much?"

This guilt increased so much that he could not carry the burden any longer. That day, he repented. He prayed and promised God that he would never steal his grandmother's pomegranates again. He felt relieved after making that decision, and he kept his word.

He never shared those pomegranates with his three friends because he did not trust them. They talked too much. Neither did he carry any of them to school to share with his classmates. He behaved this way to avoid any conflict with his comrades. He did not want his actions on "the pump head." The people living in that community, especially those in the enclave, would talk about a fly if they saw it excreting on a screen. The song by Joe Jones, *You Talk Too Much*, adequately expressed how Carlos felt about those people. Here are the lyrics for that song:

You talk too much, you worry me to death,
You talk too much, you even worry my pet,
You just talk, talk too much.

Back in school, he was always aware of the talking, talking. He listened to people as they talked in the morning; they talked at noon and talked in the evening. He made every effort to avoid distraction from achieving his goals by this amount of talking. He worked very hard at school and, before long, distinguished himself in the classroom.

This characteristic earned him some trouble as other children attacked him, taunted him, and tried to kill his interest in his schoolwork. They mocked him for not joining them in their activities as often as they wished. His resilience and fortitude were strong, and he refused to bow to those pressures.

However, during his third year in school, he was placed in a grade with some teenage boys who were slow learners and not interested in the subjects that were taught in the classroom. Those were the days when "the sun never set on the British Empire." As a British colony, the islands were part of that British Empire, and the education available reflected that relationship. It was very British. The education was so British that the environment in which they lived seemed unreal to them. The books used in the school told the students more about life in Britain and other parts of the empire; the songs that the students sang with passion, such as, "Rule Britannia, Britannia Rule the Waves, for Britons never, never shall be slaves," they sang their little hearts out not realizing the colonial conditioning that was taking place in their lives. They were being brainwashed into loyal subjects of His Majesty, and they did not know it.

At the same time, they were not allowed to sing Caribbean folk songs in school. Those songs were not accepted by the leaders in the community and the territory. They could sing English, Scottish, and Irish folk songs, which the teachers decided to teach them. They were told the stories of British warriors, heroes, sailors, and plunderers. The students were rebuked when they spoke the creole language in school. They were required to speak internationally accepted English. This type of schooling generated tensions between the school and the people in the enclave. In the enclave, the people spoke creole, which they referred to as "broken English."

Carlos's mother would rebuke him and remind him that he ought to speak the form of English that is accepted internationally. She never stopped him from speaking creole but reminded him of the importance of the proper usage of English grammar.

The culture of the community was strongly influenced by British institutions; the government was directed and controlled by Britain, and the churches were led by English missionaries and clergy. Even the medical and health services were managed by the British. Locals were considered second class, and success was measured by how well they could respond to demands from Britain. In this environment, the education provided alienated the people. A student would learn the height and location of Mount Everest but did not know the name or the height of the highest elevation in his homeland. It was not mentioned in the books the student used. Those books were not written by local people. They were written by strangers.

The teachers taught Carlos how the Europeans discovered the Caribbean islands but despised the civilization they met in the islands and destroyed the inhabitants through slavery and disease.

Despite those shortcomings and negligence in education, Carlos succeeded in getting a good foundation in English, which paid off in future years. He can still recite passages from poems and plays he studied during those colonial days.

One can understand why these teenage boys showed no interest in those activities, which were far removed from their agricultural life. What troubled Carlos while in that grade with those boys was that he was becoming a victim of their disturbances, distractions, and lack of interest in school activities. He tried to ignore them, but they would still interfere with him. After a few weeks, two of them insisted that he assist them with their assignments and threatened him if he refused to carry out their instructions or if he reported their request to anyone. He was forced to comply because he did not have an older brother to defend him, and his friends from the enclave were no match for those guys. The relationships went well, but Carlos felt like a prisoner. He was concerned about the way those boys were deceiving themselves by cheating. Before attending school, his mother taught him that cheating was sinful and one who cheated was robbing himself. If any student was caught cheating at school, the penalty was great, usually corporal punishment.

Carlos excelled in his studies, and each day he found school more interesting and meaningful. Of course, there were a few things he did not like about school. The headmaster used his leather strap very often, punishing students all through the day for little misdemeanors. It was mentioned earlier that if a student arrived at school late, he was punished. He recalled how one morning he was late in getting off to school, and he ran until he was tired. When he looked at his shirt, one of the buttons was missing. He stopped by a prickly pear (cactus) hedge at the roadside to break off a golden spine about one inch long to fasten his shirt. He then continued his journey to school when suddenly the headmaster, who was standing in the shade of a tree some yards away, called him and instructed him to go to his office when he reached school. His office was one corner of the building. He told Carlos he saw him playing along the road, and he refused to hear any defense. In the presence of the whole school, the headmaster rained down some blows on his back until his shirt was torn and his skin badly bruised. The pain was so great that Carlos could not concentrate on his studies during that morning session.

At noon, he went home for lunch as usual and reported what had happened to his mother and showed her his bruises. She became angry, hauled out pen and paper, and wrote a fiery, threatening letter to the headmaster. She instructed Carlos to take it to him, and he did so reluctantly because he had no choice. At the end of the school day, the headmaster went to Carlos's home to meet his mother and to apologize for the incident. Carlos believed the headmaster was under the influence of alcohol when he punished him. The headmaster tried to convince Carlos's mother that he was playing on his way to school.

Carlos wanted to speak in his own defense, but his mother had taught him not to interfere in adult conversations unless he was asked to do so. She made it very clear to the headmaster that she had no objection to her child being punished for breaking school rules, but such punishment must be administered according to the law. She threatened him that any repeat of brutality would have serious consequences. He never punished Carlos again for misconduct. Any punishment he received after that episode was for carelessness in completing his school assignments. They were very few indeed.

● ● ●

Carlos was fond of his schoolmates and shared in their successes and losses. One such occasion was the day when the news came to the school that one of his classmates, a girl whom he loved very much, had drowned in a well. Her mother sent her to fetch water from the well and, after she failed to return within the expected time, her mother made an outcry, and all the neighbors began to search for the girl. Her body was lying on the bottom of the well, with the bucket in her hand. What screams! It was a chant of voices of various pitches and frequencies, all united in disharmony. The news chilled her classmates at school, and that day they could not concentrate on their work. There were no school psychologists or guidance counselors to help the students with their grief, but the teachers were helpful in comforting them.

    The teacher allowed each student to select whatever activity would provide comfort. The drowned girl had to be buried within twenty-four hours because there were no funeral homes in those days, and each family cared for dead relatives. Many of her classmates attended her funeral and shared in the grief of her siblings, who were also students at the school. Carlos has always remembered the hymn written by John Ellerton (1826-93), which the school sang on that sad day. The first and fourth read as follows:

> *The day thou gavest, Lord, is ended*
> *The darkness falls at thy behest,*
> *To thee our morning hymns ascended*
> *Thy praise shall sanctify our rest.*
>
>   4
>
> *The sun that bids us rest is waking*
> *Our brethren 'neath the western sky*
> *And hour by hour fresh lips are making*
> *The wondrous doings heard on high.*

Carlos had several conflicts with teachers from time to time. Sometimes the conflict began with him, as was the case in this episode. The teacher was solving a mathematical problem for the class and had some difficulty with it. Carlos spotted the error and informed the teacher where he had made the mistake. The teacher took offense and threatened to suspend him from class if he did that again. Carlos was unaware of the insecurity of the teacher. Perhaps Carlos was too arrogant in pointing out the error and may have rubbed the teacher the wrong way. When the teacher threatened to suspend him, Carlos responded, saying, "Suspend me if you think you are bad."

The teacher asked him to leave the class, but he refused. At that point, the teacher stopped teaching, and the whole class became anxious to see the showdown. Just then, the period ended, and so did the episode. The fallout from that encounter plagued his relationship with the teacher during his stay in that class. Carlos always showed respect for his teachers but was always ready to counter any effort to portray him as stupid, weak, or negligent.

On another occasion, he was a member of Miss Smith's class. She was a strict but sound teacher. She explained the content of her lessons very well. She was the kind of teacher a student would have loved for her ability to explain ideas but hated her disciplinary measures. One day, Carlos's class had a written assignment, and, as usual, she walked around the class checking on individual progress. She spotted that Carlos had spelled the word "any" with an "e"—that is, "eny."

She grabbed his ear and twisted it while saying, "Spell the word 'any.'"

He said, "e-n-y"

She gave the ear another twist— much more severe this time. Again, she asked him to spell the word "any."

Carlos was confused, and again he said "e-n-y."

A third twist of the ear left it almost lifeless. Then she said, "a-n-y."

Carlos wanted to hate her for what she had done, but she was such a good teacher, whom all the students loved, that he tried very hard to avoid her having to punish him again. He was very concerned about the emphasis on punishment. He could not understand why every mistake warrants punishment. It seems to him that the teachers had a lot of anger folded up in their lives, and every opportunity to unfold some of it was welcomed. The punishment was never accompanied by hate, but a declaration to help the students to learn.

In spite of the unpleasant happenings, attending school was a pleasant experience for Carlos. The education he received at the East End School was as rounded as the curriculum allowed. The emphasis was on memory work and regurgitation, with few opportunities for creativity in subjects like essay writing and art. The community in which he lived, and for which the education prepared him, was agrarian. There were no industries except a few cottage activities in straw work, knitting, and craftwork done mainly by the women. The men worked in the fields, in fishing, and sailing the locally built boats to and from other Caribbean islands. School did not prepare the students for these activities. A few students went into teaching, the civil service, and nursing. Carlos was beginning to see his purpose in life as helping people to discover why they were placed on earth, and he decided to join the teaching profession.

The following poem, which summarizes vividly some of the early experiences of children in the Methodist Elementary School at East End, was written by Jennie N. Wheatley, a former classmate of Carlos, head teacher, assistant principal of the British Virgin Islands High School, and first director of Virgin Islands Studies, H. Lavity Stoutt Community College.

A 5-year old girl stands at the door, the very door she entered yesterday
   for church and Sunday School, Today is different!
The pews and benches are rearranged, the organ locked and covered.
The headmaster's desk, complete with bell and strap, dwarfed against
     yesterday's pulpit.
The teacher who had been the preacher yesterday
Stands stiff in spotless suit of white.
Her sisters, teachers too,

Who held her hand to bring her here now seem aloof, apart.
They open cupboards, peruse some serious books, and chat seriously with folks
 Who used to looks human.
Her other friends, some well bedecked, some poor but very clean,
 All seem lost in this new world.
 Her brothers and sisters
 Play outside , as if they know their way,
 Then the bell rings
A sound she'd heard before from home and longed to follow every day
 Children rushed into lines!
 She tags along only to discover
She is in the wrong place-Lower Division her lot.
 The headmaster reads, they sing
 At last something she knows
 From church and Sunday School
 And then the prayer:
A rumbling and mumbling, "Our Father who art in heaven"
That must be new
 All lost again!
Now boards and easels grow between the classes.
 Teachers speak, and children answer.
Those big ones have pens. They are dipping them in ink. It must be fun
 playing like that..
 Some are outside in lines again.
 They are saying and singing things.
 Just then her teacher speaks,

What is she saying?
  Oh! Something. Later for that one.
  A huge boy like her father
  Takes her slate and pencil
  Underneath the easel,
While the teacher is elsewhere guiding somebody's hand
  He writes for her.
  His writing looks like teacher's.
  Why is he here? A grade above
  With little children just her size.
  Later she would find out
  That in an all-age school
  It meant just what it said, that fifteen, six or ten
  Sat in one class
On benches without backs. The fifteen write on slates
  For ten whole years
And then were sent home illiterate. They could not read or write.
  They did not learn a skill
  They went out empty-headed.
Empty headed into the school of life. Three hundred strong!
The geniuses
        survived sometimes!
  The geniuses whose poverty
  Made shoes a rare commodity
  Where cattle must be tended
  Where parents blind
  To grim realities of life saw education as a thing
  for other folks who could afford
  To send their children to every day.

How could any genius survive
 When in a month
He may have tasted of the fount but once or twice?
And even then his knowledge thirst was blunted by gas and the gnawing of
 an empty stomach.
his mother cooled the milk, cut off the piece of bread. He ran, he drank, he ate,
 he threw away some bits.
Hid the treasured can-cup in the bush. Later he would pick it up.
 Still he is late.
The choice to go in, be punished, then learn or hide somewhere 'till afternoon
 school"
The little sheltered girl, fed and sent to school
On time, long before time, returns to a hot lunch,
A mother feeding, washing hands, straightening bows,
 The little girl moves on,
 Judged as fit brain.
The running hungry boy? No lunch, no relatives to beg'
 No bartering stand, deemed unfit.

CHAPTER FIVE
Adult Activities

Do not withhold good from those who deserve it when it's in your power to help them.
—*Proverbs 3: 27 New Living Translation*

"Kindness is the language which the deaf can hear and the blind can see." — **Mark Twain**

When Carlos's mother sent him on errands, he would always take time to observe the men at work. He paid special attention to the skillful application of their knowledge and skills to their crafts. He observed how the shipwright built a boat from the keel to the launch. There were many shipwrights in the village, and their workplaces were near the road, so it was easy to observe what was going on without trespassing or disturbing any of the workmen. He observed that the progress on building a boat was always slow because it was manual work, all done with hand tools. The finished product was always a work of art. It was almost miraculous to see that floating craft from the keel to the launch.

He also observed the masons who built houses from stones carved by nature, but they fashioned to fit the appropriate spaces. It was a fulfilling experience for him to watch the mason cut the stones little by little until he got the correct shapes. It was an experience in sculpture. Day by day, the building rose gradually toward the heavens until it was completed.

Carlos loved fishing, and he would spend extra time observing how the fishermen made their fish traps from imported wire as well as from materials made from local plants. He was intrigued by the method they used to fasten the separate pieces together, creating a work of art.

As he observed these various activities, he was motivated and encouraged to strive for mastery and perfection in his own activities. He saw success in action through perseverance as these workmen labored at their crafts diligently day after day. He observed a level of dedication to work and a standard of work ethic that characterized the workforce during the period of this memoir. Those examples were models that he emulated to keep him aiming high and doing his very best despite the many challenges he faced from his friends, Brent, King, Will, and other people within the enclave. Like Mark Twain, Carlos was determined:

> *"never [to] allow someone to be [his] priority while allowing [himself] to be their option." —Mark Twain*

His friends were not very focused on academic work even though they were skillful in various crafts. One day, all three of his friends confronted him and encouraged him to stop concentrating so much on his studies, and urged him to join them in some of their activities. King looked at Carlos and said, "You are a bookworm; all you can do is eat books like a worm."

"And you are a lamp fly," replied Carlos. "All you can do is fly around disturbing people."

King was angry at the reply and threatened to disturb Carlos whenever he found him studying. Brent broke into the conversation abruptly and addressed King, "Remember how Carlos helps us with our assignments. You should be kind to him."

"I was only joking when I called him a bookworm," said King. "I did not mean to offend him."

"Boys, let us keep Carlos on our side because we need his help," Will said. "He does not like some of the things we do, so let us accept him as he is."

"Alright, Mr. Preacher," said King. Carlos was running an errand for his mother, so he had to cut short the discussions until another time. As Carlos was leaving, Brent turned to Will and King and said, "Carlos has a very good mind."

"Oh yes," said Will and King in a chorus. "Too good sometimes."

• • •

The environment in which one lived had a very strong influence on the life of the individual. Carlos was no exception. The environment in the enclave was predominantly negative. People would always comment on any bad news they heard and sometimes rejoice in the downfall of someone who was struggling to rise above the negative influences in the environment. Carlos was always on the alert for these negative influences and avoided internalizing them. In other words, he would not allow them to condition the way he responded to people. He realized that he had to be immersed in these influences as characteristics of his environment, but he was always vigilant in not absorbing them into his character. He would identify those influences that had a positive effect on his life. God had a purpose for his life, and his priority was to discover that purpose.

"God has given gifts to each of you from his great variety

> *of spiritual gifts. Manage them well so th"at God's generosity can flow through you."*
> **—1 PETER 4: 10 New Living Translation**

Carlos was always interested in using his gifts for the benefit of humankind and not for exalting himself.

The adults within the enclave had their own routine activities from which the children were forbidden to participate except by invitation. That invitation was a gateway for the adults to pass on skills and knowledge. Some of these activities were mentioned earlier. Three additional activities were weaving straw, communal laundering, and Sunday morning discussions. These activities reflected values like cooperation, environmental protection, sharing resources and information, strong work ethic, working together, and security of one another's properties. One of the observations made by Carlos over a period was setting boundaries in any activity. The physical boundaries, though invisible, were carefully observed. If he or any of his friends happened to cross any of those boundaries, they would get a good tongue lashing and a stern warning to keep out of big people's business.

One day, some women gathered in the enclave to dye straw. As a reminder, the straw was made from the ripe or mature palm branches from the Teyer palm tree. They took off the leaflets from each palm and then dissected them into smaller sections according to the type of weaving planned. They produced many bundles of these dissected leaflets, which were usually white in color, and dyed them in various colors—red, green, blue, orange, mauve, and yellow. They started the day's work, which took place in the open air. They set a container on fire for each color. Each woman was responsible for an assigned container. It was organized like a production line. The leader of the proceedings, who happened to be Carlos's mother, examined every unit of work each one produced to ensure the quality was not substandard. They were well into the day's work when, without warning, it began to rain. In those days, there were no official weather forecasts, and the only sign of approaching rain was the type of clouds in the sky. In this case, the sun was shining brightly, and the rain was falling steadily.

The women rushed around, trying to rescue their completed work, but most of it was ruined by the rain. The bright spirits those women exhibited before the rain suddenly changed to a melancholy mood, almost bordering despair. After a short period, the rain ceased almost as suddenly as it had descended. The women lost no time in getting the process going again. These women's response to that act of misfortune reflected the resilience of the people of that community. Victor E. Frankl explained resilience as follows:

> "... *resilient people build bridges from present day hardships to a fuller, better constructed future.*"
> **—Victor E. Frankl, Resilience, 19, p. 17**

Carlos found it interesting that those women were able to lay aside their differences, and there were many, and unite for a purpose that would benefit each one. Some of them to the point of using swear words. They threatened one another, then they went to church and praised God on Sunday and continued their quarrel on Monday. If a neighbor's calf fell in the well, as happened one afternoon in the enclave, everyone flocked to the well to help pull it out. Everyone was in unity. Helping one's neighbor to save the calf was a higher form of service than chipping away at relationships with spicy words. Carlos found it very challenging to understand those people who this morning would bless you and by evening would crucify you. If two of them quarreled today, and a child of either one refused to greet the other one, that child would be reprimanded for meddling in big people's affairs. Life within the enclave was filled with piercing contradictions.

Similar characteristics were evident in other communal activities some of the women performed periodically. One such activity was communal laundering. The women rose early on the day of the laundering, and by dawn, they were on their way to the day's work. The activities took place in one of the small ravines where water flowed for several months of the year. Each woman carried her clothes to be laundered, the accessories for laundering, and a packed lunch. At the laundering site, each woman selected a suitable spot to do her laundering. The water was collected from the clear pools, which were trapped between the rocks. The first stage of the laundering was rubbing the clothes vigorously with the hand, usually against a washboard. If the clothes were made from thick fabric and were very soiled, the washer would use a brush to scrub the clothes. Sometimes the women made their own scrub brush from available straw. This straw was the ribs of the palm leaves, which were dissected in small strips for weaving. These hard portions would be twisted and folded to make scrub brushes. When the clothes were freed from dirt and stains, they were moved to the second stage, which was passing them through boiling water in order to remove any residue of grease or related substances they may have picked up. This scene was interesting. Large tins that could hold up to ten gallons of water were placed on large fires with the desired amounts of water and other ingredients. The clothes remained in the boiling water for as long as necessary. Every now and then, the women turned the clothes over in the boiling water. When they were satisfied with the results, the clothes were removed and placed on nearby rocks in the open air to cool. During this time, most of the water drained from the clothes, and any remaining water was wrung out by hands. The muscles of these women's arms and hands were as powerful as any washing machine and wringer of today. It is worth noting that the exercises that women perform in the gym today would not have been necessary for these women who performed every domestic activity manually.

The next cycle was rinsing. The clothes were placed in clear cold water to remove residue from the first two cycles and to ensure the clothes were clean. The women then hung the clothes on trees or rocks to dry. Some fabrics needed another process of adding starch to a second rinsing cycle, and the clothes were passed through this water fortified with starch. When all the washing was completed, the next stage was ironing, which would be done at each home. At the end of the day, the women returned home, ready for the next cycle.

During the day, when they were washing, they behaved as if they were on a picnic. They laughed, exchanged jokes, told stories, sang songs, ate, rested, and relaxed while they did their work merrily. These occasions were opportunities to catch up on the latest local and international news. Sometimes they would share in the loss of a community member by death. They would remember those who succeeded in special events and encourage one another by sharing new discoveries in culinary arts and the cottage industries. These happy occasions for the women sometimes ended in disappointment and sadness. A beautiful day could be ruined by rain or other inclement weather, though such incidents rarely happened. These activities took place before the community had electricity and potable water, and all household activities were performed by manual labor.

When performing the next stage, called ironing, the women used a charcoal iron called a goose to iron their clothes. This goose was a triangular iron box with the triangle forming the bottom of the goose. The front of the goose resembled the apex of the triangle, and the rear of the goose the base of the triangle about five inches wide. The height of the box was about four inches. This iron box was fitted with a cover resembling a goose swimming in the water, with a wooden handle and a locking mechanism to open and close the box. The bottom of the box was smooth like today's electric iron. Hot charcoal was placed inside the goose, and it was closed tightly. The air flowed into it through a vent at the rear end, and the carbon dioxide and other residual gases escaped through an opening at the end representing the head of the goose. The charcoal kept the goose at the required temperature between 250 and 350 degrees Fahrenheit according to the type of fabric that was being ironed. The charcoal was replenished periodically to keep the supply of heat constant as needed. Sometimes, two or three women would meet at one of the homes and would provide friendly conversation and relaxation as they ironed their clothes. This process continued until all the clothes were ironed. According to the number of clothes to be ironed, the process may take two days. This activity was the conclusion of a communal laundering episode.

References were made earlier to the weaving of straw in the enclave. That activity was one of the cottage industries that provided a livelihood for hundreds of people in the wider community. Almost every household in the East End community was involved in this industry. It was mainly operated by women and children, but men would assist during very busy times. The income from weaving straw subsidized the men's income from fishing, sailing, and farming. These were the money-earning activities in the subsistent economy of the period.

The women wove the straw in various patterns and made hats and bags of varying sizes and shapes. There were also elements of communal behavior in this industry. Earlier in the chapter, you saw how the women got together to dye straw. Sometimes, a group of them got together to weave straw and to teach one another new skills. While doing that, they talked about the latest fashions, products on the market and the daily news. Even the ground lizard and the mongoose would stand still and eavesdrop on those jolly folks to learn about the plots being made to kill them for stealing their fowl eggs. Each yard had fowls that were allowed to roam about the yard and neighboring yards. They laid their eggs in nests, which they would build anywhere and they believed was safe. Safety was not always secured, for the mongoose loved to steal the eggs. In order to cement their relationships, they would challenge one another by measuring which one could produce the most woven straw in a given period. They found those competitions therapeutic as they escaped temporarily from household pressures and other domestic challenges. Those competitions also motivated many of them to strive for excellence in other endeavors.

As Carlos observed those women from time to time and listened to their questioning and answering sessions, he realized that some of them had excellent journalistic skills. For instance, one woman would ask a strategic question like, "What do you think about making small change purses from straw?"

Then another woman replied, "I would like to see young girls stepping with their straw purses."

Then another one echoed, "Who first thought about making these little straw bags?"

This bridging question was followed by a diagnostic question from a real busybody. "What is the matter with Olivia's hands? Did you see those odd-shaped hats she made?"

Some good soul would reply with an empathy question. "Don't you think she did her best?"

Then a burst of laughter when another woman asked an entertaining question: "Why did Ella Gift throw her pantalet over the side of the boat?"

The conversation would go on for hours, asking different types of questions to keep the saga interesting.

Some women had to work very hard to help the head of the household keep food on the table. Sometimes they got in accidents and even lost their lives. One example was a woman who drowned off Beef Island one morning on her way to work. Carlos heard him telling a neighbor that a woman named Florence had drowned a few hours earlier. A group of people was going to Beef Island in a rowboat. Some of them were going to their small farms, and others were going to visit the only dentist in the Territory. Extracting teeth was a very painful experience, according to the reports of some of the victims. Extracting teeth without anesthesia was the only available method. The screams and groans, the bleeding and the aftereffects, sometimes from infections, would have attracted the sympathy of all available angels.

That morning, the rowboat met high seas and strong currents, and it sank off Beef Island. Most of the people swam to the shore, but there was one woman who could not swim. Some people tried to rescue her but failed in their attempts. That sad news spread like wildfire and was like a shield over the earth, blocking out the light of the human soul. The woman was beloved, and her untimely death evoked sadness. The memory of that accident remained with Carlos. He witnessed the rowboat bringing the body to shore. People flocked to the shore to mourn and get a glimpse of the body as it was taken away to the place where it would be prepared for burial within twenty-four hours.

At school that day, there was a lot of talk about the death. The school was situated on Chapel Hill, from where the site of the accident was visible. Each student tried to get a view of the site at a distance. The angry waves and the strong current that took the life of the woman became the subject of discussion among those who had traveled that route before. Carlos tried to concentrate on his classwork, but he could not control the flashbacks to the story throughout the day. The burial took place the following morning amidst a large company of mourners—relatives, friends, and acquaintances.

Today that beautiful, productive straw industry has disappeared. To fill the void, businesses import straw products from other countries to sell to tourists. This does not promote the British Virgin Islands; it promotes the countries that produce those items. The British Virgin Islands has moved from a producer of straw products to a promoter of foreign straw products. This is one example of the erosion of British Virgin Islands culture. Similar patterns of erosion can be traced in agriculture, fishing, land ownership, the village shop, and the Tortola boat, to name a few areas.

In the case of agriculture, up to the mid-1950s, the British Virgin Islands grew most of its agricultural produce. Small family holdings produced enough food to export to the United States Virgin Islands. In addition, to produce from the ground, livestock including cows, goats, sheep, and pigs were also exported live for the butcher's knife. These animals were also delicacies for the local lunch and dinner tables. Freshly butchered mutton, beef, veal, and pork were part of the Sunday lunch and dinner. Carlos remembered that daubed pork his grandmother used to cook. His mouth watered, and he ran to his mother shouting, "Do you remember the daubed pork, stew mutton, and roast beef you used to cook?"

"Of course, my boy; those were the days when you had good stuff to eat. But why come here to make my mouth water?" his mother asked.

"I wish I had some of that old-time meat soup spiced with cloves, thyme, onion, garlic, and chives," Carlos said.

"My son, today those items are imported, and many are laced with chemicals to preserve them, and most people prefer to buy the imported foods even if fresh foods were available. See how things have changed? We are changing too.

Carlos, let me take you back to how local produce was transported to other islands."

"Tell me about it," Carlos replied. "How were they transported to the United States Virgin Islands?"

"Do you remember the Tortola boat?" his mother asked. "That type of boat provided the service. The captains from across the British Virgin Islands had the shipping so well organized that every fourteen days, a regatta of local boats loaded with fresh produce sailed across Pillsbury Sound to St. Thomas. In addition to the goods for the market, people who had relatives living in St. Thomas would send packages with local produce to them by the sailors, and in return, those relatives would send other food items, clothing, and household appliances to them."

Carlos remembered delivering and collecting packages for his grandmother from her son who lived in St Thomas. There was also pleasure in the "Shipment," as the regatta was called because each captain tried to be the first to reach the port of Charlotte Amalie.

"Can you imagine the excitement generated as these captains used their best skills, propelled by the trade winds to gain the first position?" asked his mother

"Yes indeed! I can imagine the excitement generated, but where have all the boats gone?" answered Carlos.

"They have vanished like a recessive gene," his mother answered. "That's how we are in the British Virgin Islands. We hate to keep what we have achieved and build on it. We love to destroy even at the point of 'throwing out the baby with the bathwater.' We sell our 'birthright for a green bank.' We dismantle our cultural building blocks laid by our forebears and transplant imported values, mores, and ideas in our minds. We replaced the Tortola boat owned by locals with yachts owned by foreigners.

"There is nothing wrong with having the yachts for the new tourist industry. What is wrong is the local people failed to find a place in the tourist industry for the local boat. Hence its demise. We do not need the Tortola boat to take us from East End, Tortola, to Cane Garden Bay. We can make the journey in cars. We no longer need the Tortola boat to take us to Virgin Gorda, Anegada, and Jost Van Dyke. We have modern ferry services and large barges to provide those services.

"But, my son, let us not fool ourselves. The foundation blocks from the period we are referring to remain the bedrock of our well-being. People like Messrs. H. R. Penn, Ivan Dawson, Norwell Harrigan, Henry Creque, H. Lavity Stoutt, the first chief minister, Willard Wheatley, and Ralph

T. O'Neal, the first premier, among others all now enshrined in history, are examples of those building blocks."

Carlos was so drawn into the discourse that he forgot his appointment with Brent.

"Thank you, Mom, for the story. I will always remember it."

The adults of this period who laid the foundations in education, the economy, social development, politics, government, and family life would always be a significant part of British Virgin Islands heritage.

• • •

Before ending this chapter, Carlos agreed to share one more adult activity within the enclave and in the wider community. That activity is the men's Sunday-morning discussions. Every Sunday morning, before telephone and television were available to the Territory, when radio was just on the horizon, when people had to walk or ride a horse from East End to Road Town to perform various community services, or sailed on the Tortola boat from Anegada to Tortola, or when a woman in labor was rowed to the hospital in Road Town from East End, the men gathered under large tamarind trees or other similar trees to discuss the local and international events of the past week. In the eastern end of Tortola, there were three gathering places, Joe Rhymer Tamarind tree, Parham Town Tamarind tree, and James Young Tamarind tree. This discussion is focused on James Young Tamarind tree since the men who gathered there came from the enclave. They discussed news of the past week, forecasts, or predictions for the upcoming week and shared their work plans for the week ahead. Of course, these topics were comingled with a little gossip on the latest rumors that formed part of the local narratives.

Those Sunday morning discussions were like unofficial village councils. The men made decisions on certain issues, executed them, then reported to the next Sunday morning meeting. They discussed issues that affected the enclave as a small community, including opportunities for employment—there was no employment bureau—and upcoming trips overseas. They discussed the progress of children and young people, their educational pursuits, and their behavior in the community.

Carlos was a curious boy. He was always anxious to learn about the issues the men discussed weekly. He had to go on errands on Sunday morning, and the meetings were convened close to where he would have to walk. He would slow his pace to give him more time to hear some of the discussions. That was the only time that he would step outside the family moral code for eavesdropping. His mother was very anti-eavesdropping and instructed him regularly to avoid such practices. On Sunday morning, he had a thirst for information on the issues of the day, and he really did not see anything wrong with listening to the men. He was looking forward to the day when he would join them, but that day never came as he moved away from the enclave before being initiated into the group. His mother never knew what he was doing because he did not interfere with the meetings. The men never reported any misconduct on his part. On the contrary, many of them complimented him for his industrious behavior. He felt comfortable, without any feeling of guilt, listening to these men. He never shared the knowledge he acquired from the meetings with his friends. They seemed uninterested in what the men would discuss. It was through listening to those men that Carlos got his first facts about World War II. Names like Hitler and Mussolini entered his vocabulary as the men discussed the war news.

He remembered the excitement in the community when the news arrived that the war had ended. He heard the village church bell ringing on a midweek morning. That only happened when a church member died, and the sexton tolled the bell to notify the community. Carlos waited for the toll, but it was a continuous ringing like the sharing of joy. He paused from what he was doing and listened, wondering what in the world was going on. He was sure it was not the announcement of the death of someone by the style of the ringing. He was sure it was not a call for worship because it was a weekday. He was sure it was not for school, as was the custom because it was not the hour for school.

Periodically, his father would mention a few topics from the meetings during discussions at home. When such opportunities occurred, Carlos was very excited because he was able to extend his knowledge about many subjects. Most of the topics discussed at home dealt with community affairs like schedules of public meetings, health clinics, lectures, and new community products. Carlos did not recall hearing any discussions on religious matters except their comments on revival meetings when they occurred.

The men gathered about 7 a.m., and by 9 a.m., they dismissed and returned to their homes. Those who were attending divine worship at 11 a.m. went on to prepare for that activity while other men would perform other chores. A few of them would end up in bars, drinking and playing games. The rite of passage to join these groups took place on the twenty-first birthday. A boy was legally a man on that day and could sign his own marriage documents. If he fathered a child at that age, he could legally sign as the father. At under twenty-one years of age, his parents would have to sign on his behalf. Those men who spent the day in bars usually became intoxicated and did strange things. Carlos experienced one of those strange things while he was strolling on a Sunday afternoon. One of the intoxicated men attacked him for a fight. The man tore off Carlos's shirt and threw it in the ground while challenging him for a fight. Carlos's temper flared, and he took up a stone to knock out this man. The poor man was an easy target because he could not balance himself to stand. Carlos remembered his mother's advice to respect senior people and the penalty of capital punishment for killing anyone. He dropped the stone, ran home, and reported the incident. His parents were angry, especially his mother, who never swallowed her words. His father took him to the man and requested an explanation for what he did. The man was astonished, denied the accusation, and said Carlos was a liar. Carlos stood his ground, argued with the man until he relented. He said he did not remember doing the damage, but Carlos's story was so straight it must have been true. He apologized with tears in his eyes and asked Carlos's father to forgive him. Carlos's father was a quiet and peaceful man—so quiet that Carlos's mother named him "peace to the dead." He empathized with the man, for he knew him well and admonished him to refrain from drinking alcohol. The parting was cordial, but Carlos never forgot that incident and the threat of an intoxicated man.

CHAPTER SIX
Carlos and the Sea

"I really don't know why it is that all of us are so committed to the sea, except I think it's because in addition to the fact that the sea changes, and the light changes, and ships change, it's because we all come from the sea. And it is an interesting biological fact that all of us have in our veins the exact same percentage of salt in our blood that exists in the ocean, and, therefore, we have salt in our blood, in our sweat, in our tears. We are tied to the ocean, and when we go back to the sea—whether it is to sail or to watch it— we are going back from whence we came."
—John F. Kennedy, from Remarks at the Dinner for the America's Cup Crews, 14 September 1962.

Carlos lived near the sea when he was a boy and an adolescent. The sea became a part of his life, as reflected in that opening quotation by John F. Kennedy. When his teacher introduced the following poem, *Sea Fever* by John Masefield, to his class, he was so excited that he memorized it in a few days:

I must go down to the seas again, to the lonely sea and sky,
And all I ask is a tall ship and a star to steer her by,
And the wheel's kick and the wind's song, and the
white sail's shaking and a grey mist on the sea's face,
and a grey dawn breaking.

2

I must go down to the sea again, for the
call of the running tide
Is a wild call and a clear call that may not be denied;
And all I ask is a windy day with the white clouds
flying, And the flung spray and the blown spume,
and the seagulls crying.

3

I must go down to the sea again, to the vagrant gypsy
life, To the gull's way and the whale's way where the
winds like a whetted knife; and all I ask is a merry
yarn from a laughing fellow-rover
And a quiet sleep and a sweet dream when
the long trick's over.

—John Masefield, Sea Fever, Selected Poems

Carlos was curious about the importance of the sea in the lives of the enclave's inhabitants and the wider community. He showed that curiosity through specific examples in previous chapters. However, because he was so passionate about the sea in the lives of the people around him, he is devoting this chapter on this highway to the survival of British Virgin Islanders since emancipation from slavery in the early nineteenth century. The following quotation by Queen Elizabeth I of England to the Spanish ambassador in 1580 reminded Carlos of the sea's universal use:

> *The rise of the sea and air is common to all; neither can a title to the ocean belong to any people or private person, forasmuch as neither nature nor public use and custom permit any possession thereof.* — **Queen Elizabeth I letters**

Everybody in the enclave has had access to the sea, which had been a source of food for centuries. Carlos had listened to conversations among men and women as they discussed the dependence of British Virgin Islanders on the sea. The sea produced local foods, including tropical reef fish, sea snails like conchs and whelks, marine crustaceans like rock lobster and crabs, and various species of sharks and eels, and the marine reptile, the turtle. Most of these animals formed part of the daily cuisine of British Virgin Islanders from the very first inhabitants before the Europeans entered the lives of those indigenous people centuries ago. Each young boy in the enclave was the owner of fish traps they set in the harbor. This was a hobby in which most of them indulged on a weekly basis. The harbor was a breeding ground for many of these species of fish. These early experiences prepared the boys for commercial fishing later in life. Many became full-time fishermen.

Carlos remembered one day after school when he caught a shoal of young groupers in his fish traps. His excitement over the colors of those fish, as well as their numbers, overwhelmed him. He was so excited that he called his friends, who were in the vicinity, to share his excitement. Each of his friends got a share of the fish. That evening, Carlos had plenty of fish to clean, but he enjoyed the labor. He also had a similar experience with young lobsters. After lobster eggs are hatched, the baby lobsters remained in sheltered places among the roots of the mangrove trees along the shore and under rocks. When they are about four years old, they swim around in shallow water before wading into the deep. They usually swim around in a group called a "risk." It was one of those risks that Carlos caught in his trap.

During that period of Virgin Islands life, lobster was not a delicacy like fish, so children would roast them on the beach and eat them for pleasure. These experiences helped Carlos appreciate the wonders of the sea with greater interest. They also provided opportunities for him to acquire some culinary skills, especially how to prepare lobster, conchs, and whelks for the table. Many British Virgin Islanders who had lived in other countries had developed a love for these crustaceans. When they returned home, they displayed the same interest in this food item. Gradually the attitudes to lobsters as a prized food item became part of the cuisine.

These kinds of seafood formed a significant part of the staple diet of enclave inhabitants. Every household made sure it had access to fresh fish. Sometimes, if the weather was inclement, there would be no fresh fish. In such cases, the housewives would resort to what was called "corned fish." That was nothing more than salted fish. However, "corned fish" distinguished locally salted fish from imported salted fish, which was called "salt fish." The imported salt fish was usually salted cod from North America, and it was not a favorite in the enclave. This fish was a favorite item in "jail food," the food prepared for prisoners. If children ate salt fish and it became known at school, they were harassed and teased by their schoolmates. People looked down on or despised salt fish but not corned fish. That cultural distinction continues to live on throughout the centuries.

In addition to being a source of food, the sea was a connecting highway between islands within the British Virgin Islands archipelago as well as other Caribbean islands, from Cuba in the northern Caribbean to Trinidad in the southern Caribbean. Many decades before the Tortola boat was driven by engines, those boats sailed the blue Caribbean Sea, carrying passengers from one island to another, as well exports to other islands and, in return, brought imports. On certain trips, the boats would visit the French island of St. Bartholeme (St. Barts) and purchase large bundles of white straw for making hats and bags. The women who were employed in the cottage straw industry waited for this straw with great expectation.

Men from across the British Virgin Islands went to the Dominican Republic during the early decades of the twentieth century to work in the sugar industry. They traveled by larger boats called schooners, the largest of which could carry several hundred people. These men worked as engineers, carpenters, and masons, as well as cane cutters. That wave of emigrants developed special ties with the Dominican Republic as families were created through unions between British Virgin Islanders and citizens of the Dominican Republic. Those ties have continued indefinitely, and many of the children from those unions have made their homes in the British Virgin Islands. As a result of these movements, the British Virgin Islands society has been evolving with bilingual characteristics. Both English and Spanish are spoken throughout the community.

There were many maritime accidents during these trips abroad. The most famous one is the loss of the *Fancy Me*, which was shipwrecked on a return voyage from the Dominican Republic in 1926. This tragedy occurred during the hurricane season, which began in June and ended in November. This schooner was caught in a severe hurricane and failed to survive the storm. Many lives were lost, and this loss affected the economy of the British Virgin Islands heavily because the workers who were returning home were traveling with the earnings from the duration of their stay in the workforce of the Dominican Republic. Many families were already planning for investments in constructing their homes, starting small businesses, and buying real estate. All these plans ended with the tragedy. Another sea tragedy was the loss of the boat named *The Perseverance* as it traveled from Tortola to St. Thomas. Thirteen family members from the village of Long Look died in that tragedy. However, those tragedies did not weaken the resilience of British Virgin Islands seamen. "They [possessed] an inner psychological space that protected the survivors from the intrusions of abusive others." (*Resilience*, HBR Emotional Intelligence

Series p.9). They continued to sail the high seas in order to provide support for their families.

As mentioned earlier, the Tortola boat was built by men since emancipation from the grueling cruelty of sugarcane slavery. The unique characteristics of this type of boat enabled it to sail swiftly, driven by the wind. The shipwrights who built these boats became famous throughout the Caribbean and beyond. The British Virgin Islands depended heavily on these boats for their survival.

One of Carlos's uncles, who lived in the enclave, was one of those shipwrights who built many boats. Carlos had the privilege of being one of his uncle's apprentices for several years. His uncle taught him how to identify the correct tree from which he could cut timbers for the frame of a boat. He cautioned Carlos not to kill a tree in order to get timbers. He would talk to the trees as if they could hear him. He would apologize to a tree for cutting a branch and inflicting a wound on it. Carlos was impressed with his uncle's behavior, and he never forgot those lessons.

This caring for trees had an indelible effect on Carlos's growing interest in trees. He enjoyed the journey of building a boat from the keel to the launch. The day that new boat floated in the sea, Carlos felt a sense of accomplishment. It was a fulfilling journey for him. He was ready to face the powers of the sea, its ability to be peaceful, placid, and when it was ready to flex its giant muscles through the waves. These experiences helped the shipwrights develop engineering skills as they learned how to build boats with the least resistance to the wind. They learned the art of building boats that were able to negotiate smooth sailing with the waves. The design of these boats was the genius of these shipwrights. They never drew a physical plan of a boat. The plan was drawn in their memories, and they translated that mental picture into physical form without any intermediary support. They knew when a timber or a plank was not aligned or plumed with the design they were seeing. Carlos was always fascinated with the graceful movements of these boats through and over the waves.

The ability of the men to build and sail these boats was a testimony to the resilience of British Virgin Islanders to survive a period of history when life in these islands was very tough. There were few compasses available; there were no engines; a red lantern and a green lantern hung on the stays; port and starboard were used at night to avoid collision with other boats. There was no inbuilt kitchen, but the organized caboose provided the sailors with meals on every voyage. There was no fancy cabin, but a partitioned section of the area above the bilge in the stern of the boat provided sleeping accommodations. The ballast, which was usually specially selected stones polished by the ocean waves along the shore, were placed neatly in the bilge of the boat to keep it balanced and prevent it from capsizing. The ballast was in the bottom of the cargo hold, but when there was no cargo available, this area provided added sleeping accommodations.

This type of activity was an integrated thread in the cultural tapestry of the British Virgin Islands during this period. The community rejoiced with pride whenever a shipwright completed one of his masterpieces. It was a community celebration. Each person felt a sense of attachment, a feeling of part of the achievement of the shipwright.

The finished product was not pulled off an assembly line. It was the sweat and hard labor, day after day, toiling in the heat of the sun, the cool of the morning, the dry trade winds, the tropical downpours, six days a week, from sunrise to sunset. In the subsistence economy of the day, people labored daily at whatever activity they chose to perform and so they could identify with one another in their struggles to survive. Each accomplishment was a victory over the forces of nature which halted or interrupted their progress, sometimes temporarily other times permanently, as they toiled on. This achievement was also a certification that the individual had completed and achieved a level of proficiency that would attract orders from the public in the British Virgin Islands as well as other Caribbean islands.

The sea also provided pleasure for everyone, young and old. Carlos mentioned earlier how young people learned to swim, dive, and sail and rowboats, among other activities. His three friends from the enclave were "water dogs." They understood how to negotiate the waves and the currents as they swam swiftly across the harbor from time to time. Carlos was not as proficient as they were in swimming because he always had a fear of the sea even though he loved the activities in which he was engaged. There were no trees to hold on to, and that feeling of insecurity underlined all his sea adventures.

He also believed that he was always trespassing when he entered the territory of marine life. Marine animals had every right to defend themselves against human intrusion. Sharks were very common in the area where people swam for pleasure, and other large fish like the barracuda were always ready to attack. One afternoon, Carlos's friends and some other boys were swimming in the harbor, and they ventured beyond the boundaries set by the community. While they were swimming around and enjoying themselves, a shark appeared on the scene. The boys were unaware of the impending danger.

Everyone on the shore shouted in chorus, "Shark! Shark! Shark!"

The boys began to swim toward the shore, but they were surrounded by two sharks, swimming rapidly and circling around them.

The sharks probably said, "Thank you, Lord, for this meal we are about to receive."

The fishermen on the shore saw the impending attack, so they jumped into two boats and rushed to rescue the boys. The men first chased the sharks with their oars, helping the boys escape. That incident became a village affair, and Carlos's friends were punished for violating the unwritten code for sea-bathing in the area. On occasions like this, any resident in the enclave could punish the boys.

That experience increased Carlos's fear of the sea, and he became more cautious when he went to swim. Still, the incident did not deter those "water dogs." They continued to defy the sharks and any other marine predator. Carlos's interest in sharing this episode is to reinforce in your minds that the sea was a friend and an enemy at the same time. If people used it well, it was their friend, and when they abused it, it became their enemy.

Carlos tried to put that lesson into practice in other situations. He would always try to turn his enemies into friends. He used to hear his mother say that people should always do good to those who hate them. That was a bitter pill for Carlos to swallow sometimes, but it turned out to be true. Whenever he reached out to anyone who hated him, he was able to win their confidence when they perceived that he was genuine in his behavior. That was the glue that held him to his three friends. They would always accuse him of being proud, but he never got angry with them. He continued to show them genuine love and would always help them in times of difficulty. Their marine activities helped to cement their relationships.

Pleasure sailing was a pleasant pastime for some people, and Carlos loved to be engaged on such occasions. A group of people would embark on a boat and sail among the islands for a day. They might host a picnic on an uninhabited island or beach on Tortola, the largest island in the archipelago. They would swim, dive, pick whelks, or gather any other marine creature that was suitable for food.

Another form of pleasure sailing was boat racing, especially on special holidays. One such holiday when boat racing provided excitement and entertainment for people of all ages was August Monday, the first Monday in August, when black people in the Caribbean celebrate their freedom from slavery. Before 1954, when the current August Festival started, boat racing was one of the main forms of entertainment, especially for men on August Monday. The races started in Road Town, eight miles away from Carlos's home, and the boats would sail to the southeast around Round Rock and return to Road Town. Men would follow the races on land, climbing hills shouting, betting, and drinking as they traveled to East End. Each one had his favorite boat, and the shouting and rejoicing would shift from individual to individual as the boat would overtake one another throughout the race. After the races, celebrations in Caribbean style followed with dancing, eating, and drinking.

Carlos learned to observe the sea as if was a laboratory. He heard stories relating to this activity from his parents and grandparents. Some people experimented with growing fish, lobsters, and other crustaceans in enclosures known as kraals, as well as specially designed traps. They also studied the growth of these sea creatures in their natural habitats among the roots of the mangrove trees, which provided protection and nutrients for the young ones. During these periods of observation, one had the opportunity to learn which species would live together and which ones were predators. A great number of studies had been carried out on fish poisoning— and species of fish famous for causing it. The local people have developed their own folk insights into the species that have caused fish poisoning over several generations, and they avoided eating them.

Another area of interest to Carlos was the use of the sea in folk medicine. He heard many stories about the various medicinal properties of the sea from his mother, his grandmother, and his two guardians, who always looked out for him. He also remembered how older people would send their children who had a cough to the seashore to drink three mouthfuls of seawater. They would instruct the children to catch the water after the wave has broken on the shore and the water was receding into the ocean. It was alleged that you would not get any cure if you did not follow the instructions carefully. Carlos was sent to the shore to try that remedy several times as a young boy. He was not sure of the cure, but he did remember the water-induced vomiting which cleaned his stomach. The cough usually lingered for a while and then disappeared.

People who suffered from pains in their joints would go into the sea for a bath and allow the waves to massage their bodies, especially the painful areas. Many people have reported getting relief from their pains after taking these baths. Others used sea moss to wrap around the painful joints and reported that they got relief from their pains. Gargling warm seawater for sore throat was a remedy used very often by people in the enclave and in the wider community. The popular belief was it cured the sore throat.

The sea was even helpful in keeping animals free from parasites like fleas and ticks. In addition to the use of chemicals to keep the bodies of these animals clean, frequent baths in live seawater also killed those parasites. Carlos loved to perform these chores. Whenever he went to the beach, he carried his two dogs to get their baths. They also got exercise by swimming offshore to collect items thrown in the sea by Carlos. During the rainy season, mosquitoes multiply rapidly. Sometimes they attacked the animals in large numbers in search of blood to develop their eggs. It was observed on a few occasions that swarms of mosquitoes attacked herds of goats as they grazed quietly. The attacks were so fierce that the herds headed for the sea to get rid of these parasites.

Carlos shares these experiences involving the activities on, and uses of, the sea because all of them have been a part of his life directly and indirectly. He fell in love with the sea before he was introduced to its vast resources and multiple effects on the lives within the enclave. He spent many hours during his boyhood days meditating on the creative force behind the sea and the beauty of its graceful movements as it messaged the beaches and sculptured the rocks along the rocky shore. He was influenced by providence and culture as he tried to find his purpose in life.

CHAPTER SEVEN
Hurricanes

I am always amazed at how "we the people" come together to assist one another during the hurricane season or any other calamity. The beauty of human compassion always staggers me and reminds me of how divine we truly are. However, it shouldn't take a disaster natural or otherwise, to remind us of our collective humanity. —**Sabrina Newby**

Carlos heard his parents, paternal grandparents, and many of the neighbors talk about those strong, dangerous storms called hurricanes, which they have experienced or heard their parents talking about. He became interested in learning more about these hurricanes. There were no radios, television, or internet, so his sources were senior citizens, books, and observations of natural phenomena.

His grandmother told him how her family escaped during the famous 1924 hurricane that destroyed most of the island's agriculture and natural vegetation, along with hundreds of homes. She told him that the house where they lived was on a hill, and after the hurricane made landfall, the house began to shake and move on its foundation. This happened during the night, and it was very dark; one could not see anything outside. They decided to brave the storm and move to their neighbor's house, which was not as exposed. They could only hear the breaking, cracking, and falling of trees and debris, but they could not see anything.

Sometimes the wind sounded like a wailing woman, a whistling man, a singing girl, or a crying child. The only light came from the almost-continuous flashes of lightning. Before they left for their neighbor's house, they tied themselves to one another with a rope around the waist to prevent anyone from being blown away by the wind. They started walking by faith, when an extra-strong gust of wind suddenly came down, and two people fell to the ground. Carlos's grandmother had a baby in her arms, and the wind took it away from her.

After a long struggle, moving at a snail's pace, they reached the neighbor's house exhausted, mourning the loss of the baby. All the men decided to brave the storm and go out in search of this child. The darkness engulfed them. They attempted to walk with a lantern, but the wind blew it out before they started on their mission. They listened keenly in the howling wind to hear the child's cries. Sometimes, the rapidly moving wind sounded like the cries of the child. After about an hour of searching, they heard the wee voice they were listening for. With joyful hearts, they tried desperately to locate and rescue the child from a thick growth of bush strewn with litter by the hurricane.

When at last they held the child in their arms, they were surprised to discover that the child was unharmed except for a good drenching from the rain. They hurried back to the house with the good news. When they arrived, there was great rejoicing and praying. Yet, it was mingled with fear of the impending destruction. His grandmother also told him about the damage to buildings, boats, and animals. The church where Carlos worshiped and attended school was also severely damaged in that hurricane.

His grandmother's story further heightened his interest in this natural phenomenon. In addition to gathering information about past hurricanes, he wanted to experience what a hurricane was like.

Through his research, he found out that hurricanes affected life in the British Virgin Islands in the following years: 1780, 1819, 1837, 1852, 1866, 1867, 1871, 1876, 1889, 1894, 1899, 1916, 1922, 1924, 1931, 1932, 1950, 1956, and 1960. Some of the hurricanes did more damage to the islands than others. The 1837 hurricane almost wiped out the early education efforts of the Methodist and Anglican churches. The Methodist churches at East End and West End were destroyed, and Jost Van Dyke School had to be closed due to lack of funding. The Anglicans closed St. Phillips school and turned it into a refuge center for victims of the hurricane.

When Carlos discovered this information, he attempted to discuss it with his three friends, but they called him a "hurricane freak." They had little or no interest in the difficulties their forebears encountered in laying a foundation for them. Carlos wanted to understand the sufferings, the tears, sweat, triumphs, the injustice, and other challenges his people had to endure. He wanted to empathize with them to help build a better society. His friends were lovers of material things, and the profit motive had begun to take root in their lives. Carlos was leaning toward selfless desires. This was one of the differences between Carlos and his friends and contributed to their bittersweet relationships.

Carlos's desire to learn about the effects of hurricanes on the lives of his people in the enclave continued with greater intensity in the wake of his friends' ridicule. The losses from the 1867 hurricane were deeply seated in the minds of senior citizens. The stories he heard motivated him to pursue his interest. This hurricane was the most destructive one to have made landfall on the British Virgin Islands up to the time of Carlos's inquiries. He talked to his grandfather, who was born in 1875, eight years after the hurricane, and his grandmother, who was born in 1879, twelve years after the hurricane. Both remembered some of the scars from the blows inflicted on the land. The frames of wooden houses were standing all over the islands. Many people were unable to rebuild for very long periods. One eyewitness account of this hurricane is as follows:

> *"It seemed as if a total dissolution of nature was taking place. The roaring of the sea and wind, fiery meteors flying about in the air, the prodigious glare of almost perpetual lightning, the crash of falling houses, and the ear-piercing shrieks of the distressed were sufficient to strike astonishment into angels."*
> — **Hamilton**

Another source said:

> *On Tortola a hundred people had lost their lives and barely a house or building had been left standing. The small island boats were littered on the shoreline like driftwood and the beautiful palm trees were left decapitated and pointing to the sky.*

The president of Tortola, Sir Arthur Rumbold (representative of the British government and head of the colony), sent a dispatch to the Colonial Office in London on October 31, just two days after the hurricane. The following extract from his dispatch was published in the newspaper, *St Thomas Times*:

> *Rumbold the President of Tortola to the Duke of Buckingham October 31 1867 My Lord Duke, it is my painful duty to acquaint your Grace that a terrific hurricane burst over these islands yesterday. The storm lasted from 11 am to 3 pm, but the greatest force was from 12.00 to 2.00. In that*

brief space of time two thirds of miserable tenements of the town were blown away; the gaol is destroyed; the church, the hospital, pier, schoolhouse, Wesleyan chapel, and poor houses are also destroyed, and my own dwelling uprooted and rendered uninhabitable. The loss of life cannot, yet, be correctly ascertained. I have, however, already been officially informed of above 12 deaths in the town, two on Peter Island, two at the West End, while I hear that a quantity of people are killed in other parts of the country, and scarcely a hut, or habitation is left standing. All was bright and verdant; the withering blast has passed over it, and not a fruit or other tree remains. The works of the few remaining estates are destroyed. . . .

A few days later, November 12, Sir Arthur sent the following letter with more accurate and greater details of the damage to the islands:

Sir, with reference to my dispatch separate to October 31, I have now the honour to report that in the town of Rode Town consisting of 123 houses 60 have been destroyed, except for the one hired for public offices; 24 are severely and 29 partially damaged. In the country parts of Tortola most of the dwellings of the labouring population have been swept off the face of the land, all the sugar works, except two, are destroyed; all the crops are blighted. The only country residence that was left in Tortola, Ives Hall, is entirely carried away. 37 persons have perished viz 23 in Rode Town, 6 in Spanish Town, and 2 on Peter Island. After the cessation of the hurricane the face of nature, as by miracle transformed; it appears as if winter had visited the Tropics, for the few trees that stood and all vegetations were withered by the desolating blast. Anegada has escaped with little or no damage and forms an exception to the tale of woe. I hoped to be able to visit the different islands on Captain Vessey's return from St. Thomas in her Majesty's ship Doris but an overwhelming pressure of business has kept me on Tortola. The Colonial Secretary, Mrs. Porter, has been of the greatest help to me, but all the other officials are old and infirm, and there are few persons of intelligence on whom I can call for assistance in such a crisis and my presence has, therefore been indispensable. About one hundred houses are reported as being destroyed on Virgin Gorda, and considerable destitution prevails there. I had not a boat at my disposal to send supplies immediately after the arrival of the, schooner sent to our relief by your Excellency and as Mr. H. R. Semper the scripture reader and only resident Magistrate of Virgin Gorda reported to me in Privy Council that there was no immediate occasion for dispatch of provisions, I prepared a supply to be forwarded by him on his way back from St Thomas. Captain Vasey however arrived before Mr. Semper's return and I arranged with him that he should proceed thither at once and give temporary assistance.

From Jost Van Dyke twenty-five houses are said to have been destroyed according to a statement which was furnished to Captain Vasey by some of the inhabitants. I very much regret that the impossibilities of procuring a boat caused some delay in supplying them with provisions, but it was reported to me that some of their boats had escaped and kept running to St Thomas instead of coming here, it was evident that relief was not urgently required there. I have sent a supply since they received the stores from Her Majesty's Ship Doris and yesterday I again sent off a fresh one, but the boat returned having been unable to communicate with the shore on account of heavy Ground swells, the obstacles which I must encounter in the transmission of supplies, and there are innumerable and most exorbitant charges are demanded for their conveyance. I feel most profoundly misery of so many individuals and families but I am sure that your Excellency will recognize the utter impossibility of immediately supplying a remedy, I have no desire to avert the exercise of a just or generous sympathy, but everyone acquainted with the West Indies must know what gross fabrications the negro will make where he entertains the hope of gaining bread without exertion. Many who are not losers by the hurricane, and who were content to eke out an existence in a hovel rather than to labour for an honest livelihood, rush forward now with a specious tale of woe, and succeed in imposing on those who are unacquainted with their true positions and real extent of their loss. I have so far endeavoured to acquaint Your Excellency as to the damage sustained. I shall now report the measures taken to alleviate it. I have in conjunction with the Clergymen, the Wesleyan Ministers, the Colonia Secretary, the Queen's Counsel and the Treasurer issued weekly tickets for relief for food and for clothing to the extent which our impoverished circumstance admit. The Poorhouse was destroyed and as a temporary measure, the paupers have been placed in the cells of the Gaol, the prisoners were too numerous to occupy the Cells with any degree of regard to their health, but as the paupers could be placed there with the doors open the same objection as to ventilation did not exist. I have put the prisoners in charge of the Turnkey in a fire-proof store. Two gangs have been employed to clean the streets and burn the off al, also to clear away the remains of the ruined houses and to replace others which had been removed many yards from their original foundations to their former position. The Church and the Wesleyan Chapel have been cleared out and sails erected over their remaining walls so that divine service has not been interrupted. In all cases I have endeavoured to show an example as in the removal of the Paupers who were some little distance from the town. Both Mr. Porter and I helped to transport those who required assistance, equally with r to the corpses we have not hesitated to help to place them in their coffins. I entertain the hope that what has been done under circumstances of great difficulty will meet with your Excellency's approval.

I have the honour to be, Sir,
Your Excellency's
Most Obedient Servant,
Arthur Rumbold.

Carlos was overwhelmed by reports of the destruction caused by this hurricane. His curiosity was heightened. He wanted to experience one for himself. That opportunity came in 1950, when news filled the air throughout the community that a hurricane was approaching the British Virgin Islands.

There were no radios, television, or internet around and the residents in the enclave looked at the natural signs—the wind direction, the movement of the birds, the direction of the bows of the boats anchored in the harbor, the temperature of the air. There was one shipwright in the village with a barometer at his home. All the residents listened to the announced readings on the barometer and made preparations accordingly. Carlos's grandfather sent him to the home of Mr. Clem to get the latest reading on the barometer.

"Go and tell Mr. Clem I sent you for a reading from the barometer."

Carlos delivered the message and Mr. Clem, in a deep voice, said, "My boy! Tell your grandfather the barometer is down, so prepare for weather."

Carlos's heart began to beat rapidly against his chest as he became excited about the approaching hurricane. He had been waiting for this time. Without wasting any time, Carlos rushed home to tell his grandfather the news.

"Mr. Clem said the barometer is down," exclaimed Carlos.

"Weather is coming; everybody get ready," shouted his grandfather to the neighbors.

Everyone in the enclave began shouting to one another that a hurricane was approaching. They had no way of knowing how strong it would be or the approaching direction. Carlos, all excited, called out to his friend Brent, "A hurricane is coming. Is your father getting ready for it?"

Will rushed over to Carlos and Brent, panting. "What happened to you, Will?" asked Carlos.

"My father told us that a hurricane is coming, and we need to prepare for it," stammered Will.

"I was just talking to Brent about it," said Carlos. "I always wanted to see a hurricane and I am excited that one is coming."

Just then, Brent came running to tell his friends the news that a hurricane was approaching.

"Well, boys, we are going to get a hit from a hurricane," Brent informed the others with a serious countenance.

Just then, a flock of frigate birds, locally called scissor-tail birds because the tail opens like scissors, flew overhead, and everybody looked up to see the natural sign that indicated a hurricane was nearby. Those birds flew around and into the hurricane without any fear.

"Let's go home to help our parents prepare for the hurricane," Brent said. "If we have any free time before the hurricane strikes, we will meet here, under this tamarind tree, to discuss the weather."

Everyone in the enclave was busy storing away loose objects, putting bars across the windows and doors to secure them from opening during the hurricane. Every household was securing their water supply, tying down the containers, and disconnecting the gutters to prevent saltwater from contaminating the drinking water. During a hurricane, the wind drives large quantities of ocean spray inland, damaging property.

Carlos had a small herd of goats, which he cared for as a hobby. "Loose those goats," his father instructed him, "so that they can find places to hide from the storm."

Without hesitation, the goats were set free, and they disappeared from sight in search of hiding places.

His grandfather lived in a wooden house built from pitch pine wood and secured on guaiacum or lignum vitae stilts about three feet high. The stilts were anchored firmly in the ground, and the frame for the floor was firmly fastened onto those stilts with six- and eight-inch galvanized pegs. His grandfather, in preparing for the hurricane, would tie a rope to a stilt on one side and then pass it over the roof of the house and fasten it to a stilt on the opposite side. The residents would laugh at him as he tied his house, but he was unconcerned about their mockery. Everyone secured food supplies that would last for two days and waited for the hurricane to make landfall. Fortunately, in this case, the hurricane did not strike directly, and little damage was done to properties, and no one was injured.

During the hurricane, all the children at Carlos's home huddled together and listened to the howling wind and the rain falling on the roof. Carlos was scared even though he was very excited before the hurricane made landfall. He tried to be brave and to comfort his siblings while his father and mother sat calmly, chatting about the storm and walking around now and then to make sure that there was no damage to the house. The hurricane lasted about six hours. After it had passed, everyone came outside to view the damage to property, which was less than the residents expected. Everyone thanked God for taking them through the storm.

Carlos ran over to Brent's home to see how they were doing.

"Hi, King. How did you ride out the storm?"

"I slept through most of the storm," Brent replied. "The others kept awake, eating and laughing and chatting."

Carlos declared that he was a little scared, but he felt comfortable with his siblings. Brent and Will came running to share in the joy of escaping any damage.

"Are you going to write about the hurricane?" Brent said to Carlos.

"Perhaps next week," said Carlos. "For now, I am going to help my parents clean up the debris."

This task took two days to complete. Within a few days, things were back to normal.

Carlos also remembered helping his mother with the preparations for Hurricane Betsy in 1956. This time he had to play a leading role in the family because his father and grandfather had already died. The hurricane passed close to the British Virgin Islands and, again, very little damage was done. The island of Puerto Rico, which is just sixty miles northwest of the British Virgin Islands, received some heavy damage and sixteen lives were lost. After this hurricane passed, Carlos and his friends joined with other residents and cleaned up the enclave. This was an opportunity for Carlos to tell his friends about the protecting hand of God, who had spared their lives. As usual, his friends did not give him their attention because they were not Christians.

During the next decade, the hurricanes traveled along paths that took them away from the British Virgin Islands. The 1956 hurricane, which came close but did not make a direct landfall, was another wake-up call. The residents became more conscious of the dangers of hurricanes and began to build concrete houses that would withstand these heavy storms. Carlos's curiosity was further tested in 1960, when Hurricane Donna passed very close to the Virgin Islands, causing some serious damage to the northernmost island of Anegada and minor damage on Tortola and the other British Virgin Islands. By this time, he was a young adult and began to understand the fury of nature. These experiences helped him to develop a greater love for geography, and he spent many hours every week studying this subject.

Carlos also developed another type of inquiry relating to God, who created the universe. If God created people and he loved them, why would he destroy them by disasters like hurricanes? This search for answers would take him down a long path for many years, but he was determined not to give up. He believed that there was some link between his purpose in life and the need to respond to the victims of hurricanes, since he had no power to stop them from occurring. During a raging hurricane, when most people were concerned about their safety and survival, Carlos spent most of his time reflecting on how the aftermath of the hurricane would influence his purpose. He thought about opportunities that might open for him to help people who were affected by the hurricane. He spent time praying during the hurricane because he believed in the power of prayer.

He remembered his grandparents going to the local church to pray on the Thursday preceding the official beginning of the hurricane season. This was a tradition in the days before the radio. They prayed for God's protection during the hurricane season. This was an annual ritual known as the Service of Supplication. Deeply religious churchgoers looked forward to this special service and would make every effort to attend. At the end of the hurricane season, the church held another special Thanksgiving Service to express gratitude to God for taking them safely. Carlos did not attend any of these services because it was the custom that children and young people remain home while their parents and grandparents prayed on their behalf.

Carlos gradually realized he was "a walking hurricane." He had a "tiger" within him, which, when unleashed by the tongue, would destroy the best of character and defile the most noble personality. He had tried throughout his life to keep this unleashed force at bay. When he took up the stone to strike the old man who held his hat, when he attempted to stone the intoxicated man who assaulted him on a Sunday afternoon, when he fought with one of his boasting schoolmates for more than an hour, he was unleashing that inward hurricane. One of his struggles in life was to overcome and defeat that hurricane of anger.

He believed a hurricane had a cleansing effect on the environment in addition to the destruction left in its wake. The hurricane took away organic and inorganic debris from the environment. This cleansing was followed by a renewal of the individual's faith to rebuild. The renewal took place in rebuilding physical structures, renewing people's minds through searching for new techniques, new methods, and new approaches to increase their security from future hurricanes.

Carlos began to search for new avenues that would strengthen his inner self through the purpose motive, which had been guiding him when his internal hurricanes began to fire up. It was through the death of his internal hurricane that his purpose would be set free. He began to free himself from himself, a process that would take many years to achieve. He was convinced there was victory ahead, and gaining that victory was his goal. His friends began to give more serious attention to the ideas he shared with them and the encouragement he gave them.

One day, Brent said to Will, "There is something special about Carlos because he never treats us unkindly or gets angry with us even though we harass and criticize him."

"Boy, I was thinking so, too, but I didn't say anything," replied Will.

King stood with his mouth wide open, listening to his two buddies. Then he blurted out, "Are you all his converts?"

Just then, they saw Carlos walking toward them, and they pretended that they were speaking about another subject.

"What are you guys up to?" Asked Carlos.

"We were discussing what we would like to do for a living," answered King.

"That's a good way to spend your spare time," said Carlos.

"We know it is a good pastime; we don't need you to confirm that," replied Will with a crafty smile on his face and a wink of his eyes to Brent and King."

"The important thing is that you are doing something that is meaningful and not what I may say about your actions, so keep your hearts clean and your minds fertile," Carlos told them politely and continued his journey, leaving them to their own devices.

These ideas provided a platform for criticism and ridicule as well as a pathway for respect by his friends. The hate-love paradox that cemented Carlos's relationships with his friends continued to motivate Carlos to love his friends, while it remained questionable if his friends loved him. Carlos's philosophy of life could be summed up in these words by Bill Strickland:

"The value of a life can be measured by one's own ability to affect the destiny of one less advantaged."

CHAPTER EIGHT
Celebrations

"People of our time are losing the power of celebrations. Instead of celebrating we seek to be amused or entertained. Celebration is an active state, an act of expressing reverence or appreciation. To be entertained is a passive state. It is to receive pleasure afforded by an amusing act or a spectacle ....Celebration is a confrontation, giving attention to the transcendent meaning of one's actions."
(Source: *The Wisdom of Hershel Abraham*
by Joshua Hershel)

Carlos loved conversations, celebrations, and commemorations and always did his best not to miss any celebrations—whether it was for family, church, school, or a national celebration. Celebrations have played significant roles in the culture of the British Virgin Islands. They helped individuals identify with their forebears, and this bonding connects one generation with another. Celebrations help widen our collective knowledge about the community's growth and development. They offer opportunities to travel down memory lane in our lives and to venture into creative ways of interpreting the past.

Celebrations have helped Carlos find his purpose in life. He had many opportunities to interact with people of all ages and of different persuasions and faiths. He was able to recognize good from evil in these relationships and to avoid evil as much as possible. Celebrating festivals, holidays, political events, religious milestones, and other cultural activities have added color and enrichment to life in the British Virgin Islands. Carlos spent many hours recording activities for future reference and preservation. The annual celebrations may be placed in three groups:

1. Celebrations reflecting colonial rule:
    a. Empire Day, May 24
    b. Guy Fawkes Night, November 5
    c. The Queen's Official birthday
    d. Emancipation Day, First Monday in August

2. Religious Celebrations
    a. Christmas Day
    b. Easter Monday
    c. Whit Monday

3. People's Activities
    a. Boat Launch
    b. Digging a house foundation
    c. Christening a baby
    d. Wedding
    e. New Year's Eve

Empire Day, May 24

The British Empire included several colonies, protectorates, and other territories under the administration of the British government. The sovereign—king or queen—was head of this empire. Queen Victoria, who was born on May 24, 1819, became queen and head of the British Empire in 1837 and reigned until her death on January 25, 1901. Her birthday was observed as a public holiday throughout the British Empire. In the British Virgin Islands, a tiny part of the British Empire, this public holiday was called Empire Day, and schools celebrated the day with concerts, picnics, and sports events. In 1958, Empire Day was renamed Commonwealth Day, and the celebrations moved from May 24 to the second Monday in March.

Carlos looked forward to the 24th of May every year, and so did his friends. His school celebrated the day with pomp and ceremony. At nine o'clock in the morning, the school assembled and participated in a program of patriotic songs, recitations, and speeches, all teaching students and the community about the British Empire. It would not be unfair to say it was a program of indoctrination, instilling allegiance to the queen. The guest speaker was always a prominent citizen who would praise the empire for its presence in world affairs and the protection it afforded the colony. Carlos loved the songs but not the speeches. On the other hand, his friends usually felt imprisoned sitting through the ceremonies. This was the feeling of most of the students.

When that segment of the celebrations was completed, the school assembled outside the building and marched to the recreation grounds, where the remainder of the celebrations were scheduled to take place. All the students looked forward to this march, when they sang patriotic songs and waved little British flags, unaware of the colonial influences that were conditioning their lives. Carlos also loved that segment of the celebrations because of the physical freedom it afforded each student.

He remembered one year, 1949, when the marchers were singing *John Brown's Body lies a-mourning in the Grave* as they marched along the main road. Just as they passed the home of a man named John Davis, the students changed the lyrics sang, "Hang John Davis on a sour apple tree." The change generated a lot of humor and fun. His mother was angry about the song and complained and fussed, but everyone enjoyed the new lyrics, and she got nowhere with her protest. This was the activity that Carlos's friends loved, and they danced with all their might, singing and waving their flags. Carlos was a little stoic, walking briskly but not waving his flag. Many villagers lined the road to see the students parading. It provided good entertainment for them as well as an opportunity to relax from their daily chores. The school did not have a marching band, but the voices of the students rang out loud and clear, producing the rhythm they needed.

On arriving at the recreation grounds, the students were served light refreshments in the form of a drink like Kool-Aid and a bun for each student. This was followed by a free period when the students engaged in their own activities and vendors sold most of their delicacies. These items were mainly homemade candies of all types and shapes, cakes, and small tarts. They were items the students loved. Many parents volunteered to assist the school staff in preparing lunch for the students. All the students looked forward to that mutton stew, which was a delicacy at this celebration. Those women had been preparing lunch for the students all morning, and now they were ready for that sumptuous meal. Sometimes the aroma in the air activated salivary glands and started growls in stomachs.

This year, 1949, Carlos was busy observing all that went on since they arrived on the recreation grounds. He missed his refreshments, but because of his independent mind, he was unconcerned about that. However, he was not going to miss that mutton stew lunch. Disposable food containers were not available during this period, and on this occasion, the students traveled with their eating and drinking utensils. There were no backpacks, and only a few students carried schoolbags, but every student had to carry a container with these items. Carlos was very uncomfortable walking with his bag, so he persuaded an aunt who was assisting with the meals to take care of it for him until lunchtime. His friends were not so fortunate to have that assistance, so he persuaded one of his aunts to be the custodian for his friends' utensils. Once Carlos had finished these arrangements, his friends ran off to play, leaving him to himself.

When he met them again, he shouted, "Birds of a feather flock together."

Brent flew into a rage and replied, "You are jealous of our friendships."

Carlos quietly ignored him, avoiding any disturbance. He understood that his friendship with these three guys was one of convenience, but he did not allow that to foster a spirit of hate, repugnance, or rejection against his friends. He wanted them to be genuine friends, and he demonstrated that by the way he treated them. He was always willing to overlook those instances when they disagreed with him or when they taunted or even rejected him temporarily for his conservative views on some issues, especially ones involving morality.

All the students enjoyed their traditional lunch and began to prepare for sports, the last segment of the celebrations, which would end the day. Students practiced running in crocus bags, running with an egg in a spoon, running with an empty bottle unsupported on the head, as well as performing high jumps and long jumps. Carlos was interested in running the 100-yard race and long jump. He fought fiercely to get a silver position in the 100-yard, but failed to gain a prize in the jumps. His friends were more athletically inclined, and they won many prizes in several sports. The day ended with the spirit of cordiality, comradery, and cooperation. The celebration was one of many opportunities for the community to express its allegiance to the Crown. That allegiance during this period was very strong. However, there were signs on the horizon that it would be weakened through negligence by the Crown as well as the increasing influence of the US Virgin Islands.

Celebration of the Queen's Birthday

The celebration of the reigning monarch's birthday came into effect after 1958, when the British Commonwealth ceased recognizing Queen Victoria's birthday as a public holiday. It was another occasion when students, uniformed organizations, government officials, and the general public met at the public recreation grounds in Road Town to celebrate. This was a national celebration, when those who qualified for national honors were recognized. Marches to the beat of bands were performed with pomp, and a message from the Queen was read. This was another reflection of the ties between the government of Great Britain and the territory of the British Virgin Islands. Symbols of this connection in the forms of pamphlets, flags, pins, brochures, and other souvenirs would be distributed during some of these celebrations.

Carlos also loved these events. He was a captain of the 1st Boys Brigade Company, and he used these opportunities to expand his knowledge of the British Commonwealth. The spirit of these celebrations increased his motivation for civic service and helped define his purpose. The symbols from the celebrations meant very little to him. The relationships he was able to forge with members of other civic organizations and the general public helped him become the person he was destined to be. His efforts to get his three friends to join organizations like the Boys Brigade and the Boys Scouts were unsuccessful. They were not inclined to submit themselves to the discipline of these organizations. They loved their freedom and always resented anything or anyone that would interfere with that freedom.

Guy Fawkes Night

This celebration commemorated the discovery of the gunpowder plot to blow up the British House of Lords on November 5, 1605. Guy Fawkes was guarding the explosives planted beneath the House of Lords when he was arrested. The occasion was a joyful one because King James I survived an attempt on this life. People lit bonfires around London to celebrate this event, which was made a public holiday. This event formed part of the school curricula throughout the British Empire. British settlers who traveled to various colonies in the Caribbean exported Guy Fawkes Night celebrations from Britain, and it later acquired the name of Pope Night or Bonfire Night.

In the British Virgin Islands during the period of this memoir, the residents throughout the colony prepared for these bonfires annually. In fact, it was popular among young people who selected and collected the materials months in advance. The bonfires were built from logs of wood piled on one another as high as five or six feet, usually around one of the dried flowering stems of the century plant. The pile was dressed with dried coconut palm branches to enhance the flame. Sometimes, households would compete for the fame of having the longest-burning bonfire.

On this particular night, young people had the freedom to move from one neighborhood to another to celebrate the bonfires. Some reaped salt from the salt ponds and stored it to feed the fires. The flames would sparkle as the salt burned. Carlos and his friends were always united on these occasions, sometimes in a mischievous unity. They loved bonfires. The observance demonstrated how loyal the people of the British Virgin Islands were to the British Empire and its colonizing ventures. They derived pleasure and enjoyment from the bonfires, celebrating something that had no relevance in their lives. The Guy Fawkes saga was a message to refrain from plotting evil against other people, especially the leaders of the country. Carlos believed that the bad guys would always be caught, and that was a source of encouragement for him to do good to and for other people.

Emancipation Day

Emancipation Day, otherwise known as August Monday, has been observed on the first Monday in August since 1834, when the British Emancipation Act came into effect. Before discussing how that day was celebrated during this period, Carlos addressed the most significant example of freedom granted to slaves in the Western world before the Emancipation Act of 1834. He referred to the granting of freedom to twenty-five slaves and the transfer of a cotton estate of eighty acres to those freed slaves. It was a remarkable story of people without hope in the pit of despair moving to an unprecedented level of freedom from slavery to chart their own lives.

Although there were other cases of slaves being freed here in the British Virgin Islands and elsewhere in the British Caribbean, there is no other record of the transfer of land to those slaves. In this sense, Quakers and slave owners Mary and Samuel Nottingham, who lived on Long Island, New York, were unique when, in 1775, they freed the twenty-five slaves. So, when the slaves were freed throughout the British Empire in 1834, these residents of Long Look had been living in freedom from slavery for fifty-nine years.

August 1, 1834, was a new day for all enslaved black people in the British West Indies. It opened the path from the pit of slavery to the summit of freedom. In the British Virgin Islands, that freedom signaled the death of the sugar and cotton industries. It was not a sudden death, but it placed the industries on life support as agricultural activity, which had oppressed the slaves for centuries, declined. The manufacture of sugar began to decline, as did the status of the wealthy. The Freedom Act signaled social, economic, and political changes as the wealthy planters who possessed the land and the people saw the handwriting of their demise on the wall. The black people who had already begun to develop economic ties with the neighboring Danish West Indies widened their entrepreneurship, improved their skills in the mastery of boatbuilding, the famous Tortola Boat, and seamanship, and eked out a living from the land and the sea.

Thus, the celebration of Emancipation Day commemorated a major turning point in the lives of black people in the British Virgin Islands. On that day during this period, there were boat races, picnics, dances, and fetes, all designed to express thanks for the freedom for which their ancestors toiled and suffered.

In the previous chapter, Carlos shared the joy of boat racing on this day. While the boats raced, the celebrants on the land enjoyed annual picnics. They were mini-carnivals, and people traveled several miles to share in the festivities. Men and women consumed alcoholic beverages without due regard to the aftereffects. They danced, they ate, and they drank. It was Emancipation Day. In 1954, the celebrations took the form of a national festival. In 1953, the coronation of Queen Elizabeth II was celebrated with great pomp and ceremony. Everyone joined in a central celebration in Road Town. This format was transferred to the Emancipation Day celebrations the following year. People organized troupes and floats depicting aspects of pre- and post-emancipation life.

The celebrations have inspired some people to explore their heritage to find out more about their ancestral history and the journeys of their forebears. This search has been growing, and Carlos enjoyed being a part of this movement. This was another time when he and his friends were in harmony in their beliefs and their search for more information about their heritage. Carlos had strong beliefs in family ties and used every opportunity he had to learn as much as he could about his ancestors. He explored the roots of the four strands of his family on Peter Island, Salt Island, Anegada, and Tortola. He wanted to be sure that he understood who he was and why he was who he was. His existence was not by chance; it was not an experiment. It was planned with a purpose—a divine plan, a distinct plan, and a direct plan. He believed it, and he explored it. He was determined to climb to the heights of his purpose.

Celebration of Religious Festivals

Religious festivals, such as Christmas, Easter, and Pentecost, have been woven into the tapestry of British Virgin Islands culture. Long before

Emancipation, religion was an awakening force in helping his ancestors discover their gifts in the service of humanity. The church and secular versions of the three Christian celebrations listed above were very different from one another.

At Christmastime, the churches' celebrations reminded all of the birth of Jesus Christ and the purpose of his birth. Church bells rang out, Christmas trees were lit, decorations reminded all the beauty of the Christ child. The singing of Christmas carols was heard everywhere. The services in Carlos's culture were celebrated on the Sunday before Christmas Day and on Christmas morning. In the wider community, carolers and revelers serenaded the dawn of Christmas Day. The serenaders moved from one house to another, playing a fungi band and singing Christmas carols as well as folk songs. They would partake of the refreshments provided by the host family and then part with one of the famous goodbye songs. This would be repeated at every home visited. It was not unusual for the carolers to celebrate all day. The people enjoyed it, and they entertained them joyfully.

In addition to the serenading, there were house parties and concerts at various times during the season, from Christmas Eve to Boxing Day and sometimes on to New Year's Eve and New Year's Day. Boxing Day has been a public holiday, and the reveling would continue into that day. One of the traditions the people in the enclave enjoyed was sharing their Christmas delicacies—pastries, puddings, bread, freshly butchered mutton, or pork—with one another. One family would send a portion of their Christmas delicacies to a neighboring family, who would reciprocate with portions of their delicacies. The messengers sometimes had to restrain themselves from helpings of the sweetly smelling daubed pork or mutton, or the creole beef stew. Just writing about this sharing caused Carlos's mouth to water. One reason behind this sharing was to ensure as far as possible that everybody had Christmas delicacies. It reflected the spirit of giving exemplified in the birth of the Christ child in the Bethlehem manger.

While the adults were occupied, the children celebrate with toys—harmonicas, flutes, maracas, drums, triangles, and ukuleles—making their music and dancing. They would have collected their presents from Santa Claus on Christmas morning and would share their gifts with one another. The children were not allowed alcohol, so they could not drink the traditional Christmas guavaberry liqueur or the Miss Blyden liqueur. The guavaberry bears no resemblance to guava. It's more like a blueberry. Miss Blyden liqueur was made from the pears of a species of cactus known as *Opuntia*. The children ignored those restrictions very often. They had an underground system of siphoning off their parents' liqueur and sharing it with their friends. Carlos was caught on a few occasions indulging in such practices but escaped punishment because it was Christmas and freedom was greater at this time.

Easter Celebrations

The whole community acknowledged Easter as a great religious festival. It was usual for the number of church attendees to increase on Easter Sunday. They acknowledged that the resurrection of Jesus Christ opened the way for people to be saved from their sins. People who did not attend church services also acknowledged the importance of the resurrection in their lives, and they would rest quietly for that day and reflect on their immortality. Many would spend several hours reading and studying the Bible. The following Monday has been a public holiday for many decades. People celebrated the day with boat races, beach picnics, excursions, and other forms of pleasure-making activities. Carlos discovered that before the introduction of tourism, these activities were carried out with great respect for the religious observance on the previous Sunday. With the introduction of tourism in the economy, these activities became more secularized. Gradually, the religious influence evaporated until it was totally disregarded. Carlos saw some of these changes and was very unhappy about them. He viewed this change in his culture as robbing people of the true meaning of life. He participated in some of these activities, but tempered whatever he did with the religious influence of the resurrection.

His friends would tease and sometimes mocked him for the controls he exerted over his life. They believed life was to be enjoyed to its fullest and, for them, religion prevented it. He would debate his position with them and try to convince them to change their views, but he had no success. On this day, he would devote part of his time to serving a youth organization. His Sunday School, the Boys Brigade Company, or even his class from day school would benefit from his service. On such occasions, if he needed assistance and he requested it from his friends, they would not refuse him, but they would make it quite clear that they were not his disciples.

Pentecost

Similar activities would be undertaken on Whit Monday—the celebration of Pentecost, another religious festival. Carlos would give his service to his church's celebrations on this day. The Whit Monday rally provided entertainment for church members, their families, and friends. There were quite a few other cultural celebrations that helped promote unity among the residents in the enclave and the wider community. Wedding celebrations, baptisms, or dedications of young children were occasions for great celebration.

One final celebration, common during the period of this memoir but does not exist today, was the digging of a house foundation.

Digging a House Foundation

When a young man was ready to start building a house, he would notify his friends, relatives, and neighbors, and decide on a suitable moonlit night to dig the foundation. The evening when the work was scheduled was a busy one for the family, who prepared refreshments for the workmen. The project leader guided the workmen as they dug deep into the earth with hoes, pickaxes, and crowbars. As they dug, they sang work songs to keep their spirits high. During the process, the men consumed large quantities of alcoholic beverages. They would work late and usually complete it in one night. The work would continue a second night if the foundation was a large one. The men continued the celebration during the construction of the house. The next stage of the celebrations occurred when the first beams for the roof were raised. Everyone rejoiced with the owner and supported him until his house was completed.

Carlos was inspired by this kind of cooperation. It blended well with his belief that people should always lend a helping hand to their neighbors. He is not referring only to his physical neighbors but anyone who was in need of assistance. His passion for serving others increased as he matured. He believed very strongly in molding his life to serve humankind.

CHAPTER NINE
Redirecting His Life

"If you work on something a little bit every day, you end up with something that is massive."
— **Kenneth Goldsmith**

Carlos's contemporaries, including his schoolmates, special friends from the enclave, and other friends he made through his mother's associations, were all preparing to enter the workforce and find their purpose in life. Most planned to emigrate to the US Virgin Islands. They were planning to seek employment for as long as they could in that country and eventually change their nationality and live there permanently. This was the trend for many decades.

In fact, most of them believed that possession of an American green card, which gave the holder legal residence status, or a US passport, which was proof of US citizenship, was among the best achievements in life. With these documents, they could travel beyond the Virgin Islands to North America and begin new lives. Very few of his contemporaries planned to remain at home in the British Virgin Islands. This movement of people changed life in the community and especially in the enclave.

Two of his three friends decided to join this movement in search of a better life. They wanted to change their nationality and pursued this goal fervently. They encouraged Carlos to join them because they knew he would not have any difficulty adjusting to a new environment. He had a good education, maintained cordial relationships with people, and he could reason well— so his friends thought.

Their encouragement fell on deaf ears, for Carlos had already made up his mind to live and die in his homeland. His friends did not leave immediately, but those decisions began to change his relationships with his friends. They began to prepare for their departure to a new environment and entered the workforce at home in order to earn some money to help them get ready for their new dream home. They knew what life was like in the US Virgin Islands after spending many summer vacations there with their older siblings who had emigrated earlier. Their departure would change their many years of friendship, but like stars on a cloudy day, their friendship would continue.

While they prepared to leave, their attitude toward Carlos changed. They listened to his advice and ask questions about things they should have known. But, apart from that, they distanced themselves from him. Carlos was elated about the turn of events because he wanted his friends to succeed in life. He helped them whenever he could, despite their reactions to him. He really wanted to pull them out of the pit of ignorance into which they had plunged. He encouraged them to enroll in high school classes after they settled in their new homes. Unlike the British Virgin Islands, adults in the US Virgin Islands had a second chance to complete high school.

Every day, they would meet to discuss the future. Carlos was suspicious that once they had crossed Pillsbury Sound and entered the US Virgin Islands, their friendship would not continue, bearing in mind the popular saying, "out of sight, out of mind."

Carlos had to decide on his career now that his school days were past. The fond memories lingered on, but a new life awaited him. He had to continue his search to discover his purpose in life, the reason why he was born. He was equipped with the formal education that the community required for the workforce. However, there were very few jobs available, unlike today's economy, where jobs are easier to find.

He had no intention of leaving his homeland, so he worked with his father at fishing and vending craftwork in the US Virgin Islands. He would also go fishing with his beloved uncle Emile, who always encouraged him to do his best wherever he worked. The work with his father was exciting, and he enjoyed the activities very much, but there was no promise of a sustained future in these activities. He began to look deep within himself for that unique person who was living in that visible flesh. He explored his spiritual foundation, those beliefs and attitudes through which God was reflected in his life. He revisited those ideals of kindness, honesty, compassion, generosity, and love that he had shared with his friends. Every day he had opportunities to express, through these ideals, who he was, what he believed, and what he stood for. He began to see the world through the eyes of unlimited potential because of his faith in God. He believed that every challenge contained some seeds of growth, so the changing relationships with his friends was a turning point in his life. His passion for studying increased, and he continued to read and study. A quotation by Francis Bacon that electrified his desire to read: *Some books are to be tasted, others to be swallowed, and some few to be chewed and digested.*

His mother expected him to pursue a more academic course in life. She felt that she did not have the opportunity to realize her dreams in academia and did not want the same thing to happen to her son.

An opportunity for him to go to England to work and study surfaced through a very close relative who lived on another island, where people were emigrating to the United Kingdom rapidly. Carlos was not enthusiastic about this opportunity because he had already decided that he was going to live in his homeland. On the other hand, he knew very little about life in the United Kingdom, and the offer was too big a gamble for him. He was not motivated to take up the offer. His mother held a similar view. She was not willing to part with him yet. She had relied on him to assist her in her struggles, and she did not see a replacement in any of her other children. His father wanted him to make good use of the opportunity and to emigrate to the United Kingdom. He could not convince Carlos to go.

That opportunity passed, but not without some adverse effects. His father felt that he was influenced too much by his mother, and that was a bad thing for a boy. He began to blame her for Carlos's desire to remain home longer. He felt it was time for Carlos to leave the nest. Carlos wanted to leave, but he felt uneasy and unhappy, leaving his mother with her struggles. His father had his own struggles as his health began to fail suddenly. In a very short time, he died, and Carlos had to take on added responsibilities for the family. He had to rechart his course in life. The loss of his father plunged him into a world of unforeseen circumstances.

The first thing he did was postpone having a family of his own. He was looking forward to that time and had begun making plans. He now had a family to care for, and that was a challenge for him. His father's sudden death changed the whole family life. There were many sympathizers in the enclave and the wider community. However, his greatest support came from his mother's siblings, who lived on Salt Island and other parts of the territory.

Grieving continued for a while, but he had to discipline himself and accept the loss. Of course, he was at a loss himself, for his mentor and best friend was gone. Carlos sometimes felt as if the bottom had dropped out of his world. As Wordsworth said in his poem *Daffodils,* "He wandered lonely as a cloud" for some time.

Carlos continued to look within himself for an uncanny ability that would help him improvise. He believed in bricolage, using what is available in novel situations to make life meaningful. He remembered the story of

"Man Soup," which his forebears cooked in the fields. They did not have any packed lunch to take with them in the fields, so they carried what they had—flour, cornmeal, rice, a piece of salt, beef, and water. They got milk from the cows, and they reaped whatever fruits or vegetables were in season. They combined some or all these ingredients into a soup called "Man Soup" because it was first cooked by the men. Carlos learned from many of them that during wartime, they resorted to that form of cooking because food was scarce. He also remembered that some people used improvised building materials. The thatch and wattle houses, which existed many decades ago, were examples of bricolage.

This ability to improvise was buttressed by his beliefs and values of self-renewal, which made his life meaningful. These ideas and experiences helped him rechart his life. He had to develop the capacity to be strong under conditions of change and stress. He reflected on the stories that his grandparents, parents, aunts, and uncles shared with him about their survival after severe hurricanes in 1916 and 1924 when people lost their houses and belongings. In those days, the government gave very little help to those victims because the economy was too weak. The people banded together to help one another recover from seemingly hopeless situations. These situations had prepared his forebears to endure and survive hardships, to be resilient. Those positive approaches to life encouraged Carlos as he recharted his life.

A few months after the death of his father, he was offered a position as a pupil-teacher, which today would be called a teacher's aide. The position offered him not only an opportunity to work but also to continue his studies while he helped others in theirs. He felt happy because that was what he wanted to do. However, the downside was the small salary, inadequate to meet his upkeep, much less to help his mother and his siblings. He tried it for a year and had a very successful year receiving a promotion at the end of the year. The small salary haunted him. He felt like he was in a financial pit, and he wanted to leave the job. His monthly salary was equivalent to the weekly wages of each of his friends. They enticed him with their earnings. His mother, who had always hoped that he would excel academically, encouraged him to stay in the job. She admonished him to look ahead several years down the road at what he could become and not just what he is. This idea of "becoming" struck him, and he pondered on it day and night. He thought so deeply that he had dreams and visions about the future. He decided to remain in teaching and make it his career.

He met with his friends whenever they visited from the US Virgin Islands. They were doing very well financially, but they had not done anything to improve their education. Carlos was disappointed with their materialistic approach to life, but he continued to encourage them to seek those things that no one could steal from them.

When Will returned from St. Thomas on his second visit, he met with King to report on his time on that island. Carlos was preparing to visit St. Croix, US Virgin Islands, a trip he made periodically, to sell straw hats and bags for his mother and some of her friends. This was not a difficult task if the market was good, for his father had many customers who operated businesses, and they patronized the straw products from Tortola. Will, a deep Yankee (a Caribbean person who imitated the speech of an American), greeted King and Carlos with glee. King laughed so long and loud that the tears ran down his cheeks. He managed after a while to rebuke Will for "Yanking."

"Where you get that voice from?" he asked Will. "Yo sound like yo cut off a piece of yo tongue. Talk to me Jimmy Young style, boy!"

In a burst of anger, Will answered him without realizing that he had dropped the "Yanking" immediately.

"I thought you were my friend, but you seemed to be scorning me," Will said.

"Oh! No, my friend!" King said, chuckling. "Now I can understand what you are saying."

Carlos empathized with poor Will and "jumped down King's throat" with a biting defense of Will.

"You are a 'bushman,' King. That is why you hate the way Will is speaking."

King flew into a rage and wanted to strike Carlos, but he shouted instead, "If your mother was not a bad woman, I would have stopped the word in your mouth."

Will, feeling happy, turned his eyes on King and started laughing at him.

Carlos turned to King and said, "What you don't like, don't give. Remember that all of us have feelings."

"I know that, Carlos, but sometimes we don't think about the other person; we only vent our feelings. I just wanted to tease Will."

"Okay, Will; tell us about your time in St. Thomas," coaxed Carlos.

"My Son! (local expression), I had to work so hard; I really did not have much time for myself. The little job I got required me to work seven days a week. I just worked and slept."

"So you were a slave and not an employee," replied Carlos.

"Boy! I don't know what I was, but I ain't going back to that job. I wanted to leave it and look for another job, but the immigration officer won't allow that. If you stop working for your boss, you have to leave the island. I wanted the money, so I tried to stay for the twenty-nine days."

Carlos rebuked him by saying, "Had you studied in school, you would be able to do something better than caring for cows."

"Stop rubbing it in, man! Everybody don't learn alike," answered Will in a voice signaling regret.

Carlos tapped him on his shoulder and encouraged him to go to adult education classes.

At that time, King announced his departure, and all three parted in high spirits.

Life within the enclave without his father meant that Carlos had to be the armor bearer for the family, and indeed their social warfare required strong armor. He had to be a guardian, and he had to be a leader and a fighter. In the enclave as well as the wider community, child abuse, adult abuse, rape, and incest showed up periodically. Had today's laws on those behaviors been on the books in those days, there would not have been room in the small jail to accommodate the offenders. Many cases were hushed and buried. Carlos had learned about these happenings by listening to many voices in the community. He always heard his mother say, "Listen twice as much as you speak, for you have two ears and one mouth." He learned the art of listening, pretending not to hear, and not sharing what he heard with anyone. His head was filled with amazing stories about the people in the enclave and the community, but he had no intention of spilling any beans.

He wanted to demonstrate to young people that God can use anyone, even if that person thinks they're incapable of being used and other people may have placed them among the downtrodden and rejected in the community. Deep within each individual, God has planted some good seeds that are ready to germinate, just waiting for the right opportunity when the soil is fertile for growth.

He guarded his home with dedication, which surprised the men in the enclave. They developed great respect for Carlos. Many of them would compliment him for the stand he had taken in life and encouraged him "to keep his head up." This was a popular phrase used in the community. It meant striving for the best. The leadership part of his responsibilities was more difficult. Some of his siblings would rebel and challenge him. They would remind him that he was not their father. His reply was always, "I am glad because I do not have to give you anything." This response would always cause them to change their approach.

He was very strict, so strict that sometimes he ran into conflict with his mother over behavioral issues. One day, she said to him, "Just remember you are my child and not my husband." He wanted to leave home at that moment, but he could not. Something prevented him from breaking away from the family prematurely. His friends would have welcomed the opportunity for him to break away, especially King, who did not emigrate to the US Virgin Islands.

Many times, he had differences with his mother on how to react to certain forms of behavior exhibited by his siblings. He was determined not to relinquish his role in the family despite the challenges that he was up against. He loved his mother and his siblings, and he was happy to make sacrifices for them, even if he had to neglect his own aspirations.

Inside the enclave, the "crab in the barrel mentality" was ubiquitous. He could not understand why people were ready to downgrade one another and destroy their best efforts to succeed. Even within the church, a place where people should love one another, this degrading attitude prevailed. As he redirected his life, he had to develop strategies to fight these adverse encounters. His first strategy was to be immersed in the environment but not submerged by the prevailing unproductive influences. It meant isolating himself from activities that were not conducive to harmonious living with his friends, relatives, and coworkers. That strategy helped him become a stronger, more loving, and caring person.

He was cofounder of the Boys Brigade in the British Virgin Islands and captain of the First Company, which was attached to the East End Methodist Church in the village where he lived. The Boys Brigade motto, "Sure and Steadfast," and the emblem of the anchor attracted his attention and became "lamps to his path in life." Every day, he reflected on his responsibilities as a leader for those teenage boys. This leadership role provided him opportunities to understand what constituted effective leadership for the well-being of the group.

His second strategy was to be humble and control his emotions, especially anger, at all times. He practiced that so much, it became part of his modus operandi. Many people would ask him how he could always be so cool all the time.

Carlos had the opportunity to attend an International Camp of the Boys Brigade in Jamaica in 1958. It was his first trip on an airplane beyond the eastern Caribbean. The camp was held on the Mona Campus of the University of the West Indies. He joined the other delegates from the eastern Caribbean in Puerto Rico, and they traveled on an aircraft named the Vicount, owned by the British West Indian Airways (BWIA). The camp, called a "Jamboree," had delegates from every country where there was a Boys Brigade Company.

This was an opportunity for Carlos to learn more about Brigade work and to prepare himself for more effective leadership of his company. He was able to widen his circle of friends as he interacted with Brigadiers from various countries. Many of the delegates were organists and pianists in their churches and performed for various community groups. He was motivated inspired by the performances of these Brigadiers and spent many hours discussing church music with them. He was preparing for such a role in his local church. The friendships he made in this area of activity remained active for many decades.

One memorable opportunity during this trip was spending ten days at a home in Christiana with a Maori delegate from New Zealand. It was an epiphany in cultural appreciation. His life was enriched by these opportunities, which strengthened his endeavors to serve humankind with greater zeal in the future. When he returned to his home, he possessed a richer repertoire of experiences to share with his local Brigadiers as well as the wider community of young people, through his teaching in the day school, Sunday school, and other community service activities. His love for other people increased through his interactions with other racial, ethnic, national, religious, and occupational groups. That trip to Jamaica was a turning point in his understanding of other Anglophile Caribbean countries.

Today, he feels proud of the personal investment he made in the lives of those young men.

It became clear to him that he was placed on earth to live a life of service to humankind. Through serving other people, he would become the person he was destined to be. Becoming a teacher was a confirmation of that service, and he dedicated himself to the best of his ability. He was beginning to understand more fully who he was, a challenge everyone has to address. The pursuits that have energized him and brought him joy, peace, and satisfaction began to crystalize as he focused on his strengths, passions, and values. In redirecting his life, he envisioned the impact that he could have on his profession in his homeland as well as outside the territory. He believed if he worked diligently, planned carefully—taking his strengths and weaknesses into consideration—he could live his purpose effectively and successfully. He knew that he should take his family and outside commitments into consideration when he was making plans.

The more he talked about his passion for helping other people, the stronger his vision of becoming a teacher and a leader grew, and the easier it became for him to define his purpose of service. As he reflected on his purpose, the current realities of life and the prospects for the way forward began to converge as he attempted to formulate his goals for the next stage. As a teacher, he believed that he could help his students and coworkers find meaning in their work and in their lives. He believed that if his students discovered that meaning in what they did, they were bound to succeed. The challenge was to ignite that inner sense of purpose that would propel and motivate them from day to day.

Carlos knew school regulations and classroom rules had to be observed, but they were external conditions that controlled and sometimes cramped and stifled individual growth and development. If the people he worked with could develop an inner sense of purpose, that intrinsic force would empower them to work joyfully and willingly within the boundaries of the laws, regulations, and rules.

While he was reflecting on the importance of sincerity within himself, he met his friend King, who had recently returned from a trip to the southern Caribbean islands. Carlos, who had missed his friends, was happy to see King.

"Hi, King! What's the latest down the islands?" he asked.

"I was surprised to see the differences in the living conditions of so many people," King replied. "There are many rich people on the islands, but the poor outnumbered them. I gave many of them small gifts of US dollars, and they appreciated it. They were so different from our people at home. If you give one of our people a small gift that is not big enough, they get upset with you."

"Well, King," said Carlos, "I am glad that you understand the importance of helping a brother or a sister who is in need. Small gifts are acceptable to God. Do you remember the story of that widow who could only put a penny in the offering, and Jesus said it was greater than those who had given large sums? Do you remember the disciple Andrew who followed Jesus? At the end of one of his meetings with a large crowd before dismissing them, there was no food in the area, and they had no money to buy food for such a crowd. Andrew spotted a little boy with a small lunch of two little fish and five little loaves. He immediately believed there was potential in the little boy's lunch. He told Jesus about it, and Jesus blessed the lunch and fed all the people who were present. Your little gifts can be useful for helping others to enjoy something in life."

King listened attentively to Carlos, then thanked him for his encouragement. They parted with a promise to meet the following day.

Carlos was aware it was easier to follow the flow with the familiar and the comfortable. However, those characteristics did not give him any challenge. He believed that education was an avenue for overcoming many of the challenges of life. These challenges had to be addressed if harmony was going to be achieved. Today we live in an age where cutting corners and taking shortcuts have become fashionable. There is a way that seems right, but the end can be destruction. Following the paths of friendliness, fairness, and firmness have helped him to live a more successful life.

CHAPTER TEN
The Beginning of His Teaching Journey

"Everyone can rise above their circumstances and achieve success if they are dedicated to and passionate about what they do". —**Nelson Mandela**

When Carlos joined the teaching profession in February 1955, the British Virgin Islands was searching for new leadership in every aspect of public service that would inspire the citizens to aim for the best they could become. The need for security on personal and territorial levels was one of the narratives. During the eighty-three preceding years, the territory was a political unit in the Leeward Islands Federation, which came into being in 1871. This federation comprised four political units called Presidencies. They were Antigua and Barbuda, St. Kitts, Nevis and Anguilla, Montserrat, and the British Virgin Islands. The federal government was situated in Antigua, where the Federal Legislative and Executive Councils were based. Each Presidency had a Legislative Council and an Executive Council, but they had very little authority as the Federal Legislature controlled the Federation. The Presidencies were represented in the Federal Legislature by official and elected members from each Presidency except the British Virgin Islands. The representative for this Presidency was an unofficial nominee.

Between 1871 and 1902, the local Legislative Council became dysfunctional because it had no power to make laws. It was abolished in 1902, and that change ushered in a period without a local Legislative Council and a representative in the Federal Legislative Council. The governor of the Leeward Islands was now the sole legislative authority. His resident deputy, called the commissioner, and a reconstituted Executive Council were responsible for governance in the Presidency. This Executive Council was not effective because it did not meet regularly for want of a quorum. In this environment, the power of the commissioner increased as he carried out his principal duties of maintaining law and order and collecting taxes. Sometimes he doubled as the only resident medical practitioner.

Dissatisfaction with this type of government for almost a half-century culminated in a demonstration of 1,500 people on November 24. During the '40s, the United States built a naval base in St. Thomas, US Virgin Islands. Hundreds of British Virgin Islanders migrated there to work. This project continued during part of World War ll. After the war ended, these people returned home along with many other British Virgin Islanders who had emigrated to Puerto Rico, The Dominican Republic, Cuba, and Aruba in search of work. On their return, they encouraged dissatisfaction with the services given by the government and living conditions throughout the Presidency. They were discontented over the absence of a secondary or high school in the Presidency, the operations of the Public Works Department, and inadequate medical services, among other grievances.

This discontent culminated in 1949 with an assembly on the Old Recreation Ground in Road Town. There, the people conducted a religious service and then marched through Road Town to Government House, locally called "Olympus," where the commissioner lived, and delivered a petition from the people. The following is an excerpt from the petition:

"We the people of the British Virgin Islands, theoretically a free people by reason of the fact that we are supposed to be British subjects and citizens of the British Empire, are today in numbers assembled as a demonstration of people against certain conditions under which we have hitherto been forced to live. . . . One of the purposes of this demonstration today id for us to achieve a measure of political freedom for ourselves and generations of the future."
— **(Harrigan and Varlack, The Virgin Islands Story, 1975, p. 158)**

This was a turning point in the governance of the Presidency. In July of the following year, the general Legislative Council of the Leeward Islands Federation reconstituted the Legislative Council of the British Virgin Islands, and it was inaugurated on December 5, 1950.

The restoration of the Legislative Council ushered in a new era in politics and governance in the British Virgin Islands. It began a process of separation that was completed in 1959 with the dissolution of the Federation. The first elections were fought for four at-large seats. Each candidate received four votes. That Legislative Council was made up of four elected members and five nominated members. The life of that Council was four years. The second Legislative Council came into effect with the 1954 elections. By that time, adult universal suffrage had been achieved in 1953, and in that year, the District System was also introduced. The Presidency was divided into five districts as follows:

District One: Wear End, Carrot Bay, and Jost Van Dyke.

District Two: Cane Garden Bay, Brewers Bay, Meyers, and Soldiers Hill.

District Three: Sea Cows Bay, Road Town, Purcell, Free Bottom,

Baughers Bay, Belle Vue, Fahie Hill, and Huntums Ghut.

District Four: Hope, Long Look, and East End.

District Five: Virgin Gorda and Anegada.

During this second Legislative Council, another advancement was made when the "membership system," an embryonic ministerial system, was introduced. Members of the Legislative Council voted for two of their members to serve on the Executive Council. One of these members represented trade and production, and the other member represented works and communications.

It was during these political and administrative changes that Carlos joined the teaching service in February 1955. The British Virgin Islands was intent on breaking the yoke of the Leeward Islands Federation, under which the Presidency was governed from Antigua, where the governor resided. His local representative, the commissioner, did not have much authority, hence the weakness of the government. These political changes reflected the will of the people, and with recent universal suffrage, the people held their political representatives responsible and accountable for the trust they put in them.

The fight for greater political power included the struggle for better education. During the period without federal representation, there was no high school in the British Virgin Islands. Any student seeking a high school education had to go to another Presidency. Nine years of elementary education was available to students, and this was provided by the churches—Anglican and Methodist—with very small grants from the government. The people struggled long and hard for a high school, and that only became a reality seven years before Carlos entered the teaching profession.

The struggle for education reform to provide more advanced educational opportunities and more inclusion was evident throughout the Presidency. The daily discourses were centered on better governance and more opportunities for advancement in all areas of life. That included better living conditions, more job opportunities, and better education for British Virgin Islanders.

Carlos joined the struggle for better education the same year that the budding Legislative Council was able to pass the first local Education Act, 1955. The act sought to give the government greater control over education, which was provided by the churches. The struggle became hotter because the churches were not prepared to relinquish their authority. They had a strong hand, for they controlled all the schools and owned all the buildings where school was held. The first step in the struggle was to develop a partnership that would eventually lead to government control of education.

As a young member of the teaching profession, he had to learn where the church responsibilities began and ended. When he was a student, he witnessed visits from church officials, mainly Methodist ministers, and visits by government officials. It was not clear, at that stage of his understanding, what the roles of these two agencies were. At the classroom level, the students were not conscious of this struggle, and only modest interference and conflicts arose periodically. On one occasion, the head teacher requested to see the letter of authority from a government official, and he could not produce it. The head teacher refused to admit him to his school. The churches managed the schools, but the government controlled the curriculum and provided grants.

Carlos had two goals, which he never lost sight of, as the struggle continued. The first was to serve his students faithfully by helping them discover the greatness that resided within them. Second, he wanted to continue his personal educational growth and development. He wanted his actions to be a way of life and not occasional gestures. He wanted his career to be a culture that he would nurture throughout his professional life. In this chapter, he takes you into his classroom and into his study.

His first class was a mixture of twenty-five boys and girls. After considerable reflection on the task ahead, he realized that he did not have a homogenous group of students, but twenty-five boys and girls with varying levels of experiences and individual needs to be addressed. He wanted all his students to be insiders in his class so that no one would feel like an outsider and left out or overlooked. The individual economic or social circumstances were not part of the criteria for inclusion in his class. The only qualification was membership in his class. In many cases, he had helped students build bridges in their relationships with one another and with the community outside the classroom.

The students in his class ranged from those who came to school barefoot because their parents could not afford to buy them a pair of sneakers to those who could change their shoes to match each dress. He had to build bridges across that divide. Periodically, some students' hair was not groomed, and hygiene was neglected. He had to take care of these situations to enable harmony to reside within his classroom. It was sometimes challenging to maintain inclusion when the forces of exclusion were very strong. He saw this as part of his service to his students, to help them to build harmonious relationships. The more he thought about individual differences, the more challenging the task ahead became. Somewhere in his studies, he memorized a little jingle about children:

> *Together they lump,*
> *Their talents equally must jump.*

The trend to teach each individual and not the group as one was reinforced every day in the school through discussions among teachers and from daily readings. The heightened individual attention to students produced a dilemma for Carols. After giving all the individual instruction and attending to the weaknesses and differences of students at the end of a unit, all the students were required to respond to the same evaluation instrument. The best efforts of some students were not good enough to gain a passing grade on that instrument. On the other hand, many of the students completed the unit with flying colors.

He soon found out that only a minority of students were outstanding in their performance in every subject area. Other students were outstanding in varying degrees in one, two, three, or four subject areas. He developed a philosophy that every student was a success and emphasized their strengths to build morale and comradery. At the same time, he would help them to strengthen their weakness. The approach proved successful, but it was very challenging for him as a young teacher. Sometimes he wondered if he had really found his profession, or he was still searching for it. During such moments, the love for his students and their responses would change his reflections on the difficulties of teaching a diverse group of students. The joy of seeing his students mature cognitively and in their psychomotor attributes convinced him that what he was doing was a worthwhile service to humankind.

Each class did not have a classroom like those of today. All the classes used one big hall, mostly the church chancel. The interference from other classes was a daily feature at the school. It was not unusual for a student to ignore their teacher and focus on the activities in a neighboring class. Sometimes to avoid distractions, some teachers, including Carlos, would take the students outdoors and conduct classes in the open-air classroom. Under these conditions, practical work was limited as well as demonstrations to illustrate some concepts. Sometimes a teacher would take students on an environmental trip to examine natural features and record their observations, which would form the basis of classroom discussions later.

Carlos stayed at that school for four years. During that time, he had the opportunity to bring hope to many students who would have fallen through the cracks for lack of individual attention.

Many years after he had left that school, students continued to greet Carlos with appreciation for his interest in their welfare. On one occasion, he was walking in Brooklyn, New York, with his sister when someone shouted greetings from the third floor of a nearby building. The person asked him to wait while she came out to greet him. To his surprise, it was one of his former students. She reminded him of the days when she was a student in his class, and the lessons she learned had been very helpful to her. She also told him that she was doing very well. During those few moments of greetings, she validated his faith in humanity. He realized that when one sows seeds in the classroom, they can germinate, blossom, and reproduce thousands of miles away.

On another occasion, while walking the street in St. Thomas, a woman crossed the street and suddenly hugged him without any warning, and said, "Thank you for helping me to understand mathematics." He was bewildered for a while, then she told him her story. He did not recall giving her special help but did remember her as a student in one of his classes. This encounter again reminded him that a teacher should be friendly, fair, and firm with his students, and they would be his ambassadors.

He had a third response from a male student to whom he had given several hours of special help each day. After this student left school, he apprenticed himself to an automotive mechanic. During his apprenticeship, he bought a second-hand car, which he prized. One day, as Carlos was walking in the village, this young man drove up beside him on the rough road and offered to take Carlos to his destination. There were very few cars in the village, and Carlos did not own a car, but hired one when he was traveling. On this occasion, he could not get a car to hire, so he was walking. Carlos was reluctant to accept the offer because he did not trust the driver's ability. The driver insisted that he would like to take Carlos to his destination. After a brief discussion, he accepted the offer. He had a comfortable ride, although the roads were rugged. When Carlos got out of the car, he offered the young man a little money to help him buy fuel. He rebuked Carlos, saying, "I did not give you a ride for your money. Do you remember how you helped me with my schoolwork? I am happy to do this favor." Carlos was embarrassed but thanked the young man, and they parted cordially. Carlos was angry with himself because he believed it was pride that forced him to refuse the ride at first and then to offer the money at the end of the journey. This encounter was a lesson in humility for Carlos.

His second goal during the formative years of his profession was to complete the requirements for permanent and pensionable status. This was a daunting task. The system was draconian in its requirements, and many of Carlos's colleagues who were promising in this field succumbed to the exigencies of the education system. In order to achieve the status of permanent and pensionable, young teachers had to pass five graded examinations over a five-year period. Each examination was a stepping stone to the one above. The first two consisted of seven subjects each, the third of eight subjects, and the last two of ten subjects each. The challenge for Carlos was finding a balance between his teaching responsibilities, which were rigorously supervised daily, and preparing for these examinations. The tasks were made more difficult by the absence of adequate library facilities and bookstores. The instruction available to young teachers was inadequate to ensure success.

He was never discouraged by these deficiencies and found his own resources to get the required information. He enrolled in distance education programs by means of correspondence courses offered by colleges in the United Kingdom. In addition, he purchased the needed textbooks by mail from bookstores in the United Kingdom. These actions enabled him to meet the requirements for each examination. It was challenging because the time for study was limited due to the long hours of work. He did not take credit for his successes but attributed them to the power of God in his life.

After four years, he was offered a position as acting headmaster in a small school at North Sound, Virgin Gorda. This was a tipping point in his life. He would leave his mother and siblings in the enclave. He would leave his colleagues in the school where he had worked for four years. He would leave the students with whom he had worked since joining the teaching profession. On the other hand, he had to look at his future, what he hoped to become personally, what his destiny was on earth, and what contributions he could make to the development of his country and to humankind in general.

> *These thoughts preoccupied his mind as he considered the offer. He remembered a little poem he learned during his early school days, What a Little Bird Thought. The last verse reads:*
>
> *At last I flew beyond the trees,*
> *And saw the sky so blue.*
> *Now, how the world is really made*
> *I cannot tell, can you?*

This verse told him there were possibilities beyond what he could see or think about. The words of Napoleon Bonaparte . . .

> *Until you spread your wings,*
> *You'll have no idea how far you can fly.*

. . . encouraged him as he ventured out. His mother, siblings, coworkers, and friends encouraged him to take the next step and move out. It seemed that his career began to unfold before him, and he embraced the opportunity. In the next chapter, he will share his experiences in moving out.

Before moving out, he takes you one more time inside the enclave to see what life was like at that time. Many of the senior citizens had passed on, and a new generation was emerging. Many members of this generation, including two of his friends—Brent and Will—had emigrated to the US Virgin Islands. A new era had begun to dawn in the enclave and the wider community. Life inside the enclave was adapting to new changes. There were social changes through demographic changes. There were political changes, which gave citizens the right to vote for representatives to the Legislative Council. There were economic changes as people began to move away from an agrarian economy and educational changes to meet the needs of the rising generations.

Carlos was part of those changes, and having the opportunity to move to a less progressive area of the territory enabled him to be an agent of change in that new community. This promised to be an exciting time for him, and he was fired up for the brave new adventure. He knew he would be missed by the church, the school, and the enclave. He hated to say goodbye to his Boys Brigaders and members of other organizations in which he had obtained membership. However, he was ready to move on. He would visit the enclave and spend vacations with his mother and siblings, but his home was beyond the boundaries of the enclave. He believed he had a duty to make life more attractive for those who remained in the enclave, and he resolved to do whatever he could. It was the enclave that cradled him. Now he must help others to discover themselves and the purpose of their lives on earth.

CHAPTER ELEVEN
Providence Revealed

"Keep your face always toward the sunshine and the shadows will fall behind you." —**Helen Keller**

Carlos was about four years of age when he attended his first Bible class. The Sunday morning was bright and sunny, the cocks were crowing, and the hens were singing. Breakfast was finished, and he was about to set up his play schedule for the day. Without any warning, his father summoned him to a quiet section of the house and offered him a chair. Carlos was bewildered, wondering what was going on. He was sure it was not punishment because he had been keeping within the prescribed code of behavior. He saw his father with a big book, and he remembered hearing his mother referred to it as a Bible. He had no idea what that meant, but he would soon have a better understanding of that book.

His father introduces the book by name "The Holy Bible." He explained the importance of that book in guiding people on how to live. He told Carlos it was important for him to learn the rules for living from that book. His father opened the book to *Exodus Chapter 20* and read seventeen verses to Carlos. This passage was the Ten Commandments, which God gave to Moses. His father read slowly because he wanted Carlos to understand the story of the Ten Commandments. When he was finished reading, he asked Carlos a few questions about the passage and then gave him a verse to memorize. Carlos disliked memorizing the verse, and he showed his disapproval through the undertone in which he recited the verse. His father instructed him to remember the verse, which he would recite at the next meeting. All through the week, he recited the verse in preparation for next Sunday's meeting.

This meeting was convened promptly after his father returned from the men's Sunday morning meeting. He recited the passage without any mistakes, and his father applauded him. This second meeting followed the same procedure as the first one, as did all subsequent meetings. Carlos thought those lessons were punishment. He did not like the language of the King James Bible, which was different from ordinary speech. In the end, he admitted that the lessons helped to shape his life for good. Today, he still recites the first passage, which he memorized at age four.

The idea of God as a living being occupied Carlos's thoughts and imagination every day. One day, in search of answers, he confronted his mother.

"Where is God?" he asked, catching his mother off guard.

"Above the bright blue sky," she answered him quietly, reciting a line from one of her favorite hymns. Now that his mother had responded so confidently, he increased his gaze at the sky. He wanted to see God, and the more he learned about Him, the greater the intensity of His mystery.

He listened to conversations in the enclave and throughout the community. Those conversations would have a profound influence on Carlos. He developed a special interest in the things that people attributed to the wonderous, working power of God. The following are two of the stories that attracted his attention.

A few sailors from the enclave reported that, on a very stormy night while they were sailing to another island, one of the sailors fell overboard. It was dark, and those on the boat could not see him. Everyone began to panic because they feared he would drown. He was a good swimmer, and they hoped he would stay afloat until they could find him. The captain was skillful; he could read the wind speed and direction, and he had a keen sense of the direction in which the ocean current was flowing. He maneuvered the boat, taking those factors into consideration until the crew was able to contact him. They threw a rope with a white buoy at the end and shouted to him to hold on to it. It took a while before he was able to seize the rope, but no sooner than he did, they pulled him safely on board. The men attributed his rescue to the power of God.

In another setting, a day conditioned by a melancholy mood, a prominent resident in the enclave suddenly fell seriously ill. There were no medical doctors within reach, and the family thought she was too ill to travel in a boat to seek medical attention. There were no other forms of transportation available. Everyone thought that she was going to die, so the neighbors gathered at the home to pray and sing so that she would die comfortably.

Some men began to build her coffin, and others began to dig her grave. There were no funeral homes, so the dead had to be buried within twenty-four hours after death. Suddenly, events turned for the better. The woman revived and gradually regained her health. There were mixed emotions, as some relatives and friends rejoiced, while others said it was a miracle that could only be the work of the Lord.

Carlos's faith in God grew stronger as his knowledge about these stories increased. At age fifteen, he discovered something new about God during an evangelistic campaign. God became real and personal to him. He surrendered his life to God and sought His guidance as he experienced the dark forces in the enclave. There were many forces tempting him to change his focus. His friends did not believe him and tried to redirect his interest. His mother and grandmother encouraged him to pray more and read the Bible every day. He took their advice, and he felt more comfortable with his decision as time went by.

His father also encouraged him, but he died early, as mentioned before.

The loss of his father, and his grandfather two years earlier, left him the oldest male in the immediate family. He felt that he needed God to help him as he assumed the leadership role in the family. His desire for help was satisfied in various ways and in mysterious places, but always at the right time.

These experiences had their roots in earlier experiences that affected Carlos's life in elementary school. At school, he had to pray four times a day. He prayed at the beginning of the school day, before dismissal for lunch, at assembly after lunch, and at the end of the school day. He often wondered why they had to pray so much every day. One day, he overheard his mother and a visiting friend talking about the need to pray so that one would be ready to meet the Lord when he returns. It dawned on him that every act of prayer he performed was a preparation for that destiny. In other words, he became aware that he was traveling a spiritual journey. While he could not separate that journey from his total life, he chose to follow a path where he could meet and converse with God daily. A few episodes reinforced that resolution.

The first development after the death of his father was the growth in his prayer life. He organized a series of private prayer sessions. He selected a large tree about forty feet tall with thick branches about two hundred yards from home and built an altar from small stones. The area was surrounded by small trees and shrubs and was at an elevation about two hundred feet above his home. He would not be visible to anyone when he was praying. The area was quiet, so he could listen to the voice of God without the hustle and bustle of the environment.

He paid daily visits to his altar and prayed for as long as he was inspired. He was convinced that there was no one other than God who could help him through his struggles.

One afternoon, he was praying intensely and louder than usual. His grandmother heard his cries, and when he climbed down from the altar, she called him. She was patiently waiting for him, but he did not know it.

"Carlos, are you well?" was her first question.

"Yes, Granny," he replied.

"Then what is worrying you?" She said quite firmly.

"I just want to know that God is going to direct my life," he said.

"You do not have to worry about that," his grandmother joyfully announced. "He feeds the sparrows, so he will feed his children."

She gave him approval for his prayers, and that drew him closer to her. She lived for another twenty-one years and died at the age of 103.

He knew that his mother was suspicious that he was up to something unusual because she noticed his absence during the same time every day. She thought he was engaged in some kind of mischief, so she set out on her own investigation. He was not aware that he was being watched closely, but even if he knew, it would not have changed his schedule of prayers. Somehow, she found out and was more comfortable. Perhaps her revelations came through her conversations with his grandmother. He did not care about that; he continued to make his daily prayers. He was convinced that God answered him in a dream.

One night, he dreamed that someone took him to a ladder suspended in the air over the sea. The person carried him to the top of the ladder, which had fourteen steps. As soon as they reached the top, the person disappeared, and he woke up.

He was now more puzzled than ever. What was the meaning of that dream? This question haunted him for several years. He never forgot it. He was always searching for the interpretation. He believed it was one of the signs that God was with him and was preparing him for greater service. The revelation came to him during the middle of his career, when he began to succeed as an educator. He had fourteen stages to go through before reaching the top of his career. To this day, that dream has been one of his assurances that God was leading him.

Another vivid encounter with God occurred about two years later. He had traveled to the island of St. Croix in search of vacation employment. It was a bright summer evening; the sky was cloudless, and the stars lit the heavens. They looked like pieces of gold scattered in the universe. Carlos became intoxicated with the evening's beauty as he strolled down Kings Street, Christiansted. Suddenly, the strains of organ music floated through the air. This beautiful sound brought him out of his reflections on the heavens. He stood up and listened to the music for a few minutes. Then, drawn by the lovely sounds, he walked into the church from which those musical strains emanated. He sat at the back of the church. His thoughts were transformed by the pipe organ.

If music on earth is so beautiful, what about music in heaven? he thought. He drank in the strains until he was lost in the beauty of the "Hallelujah Chorus" from Handel's *Messiah* as they peeled forth from the organ. He was interrupted by a voice that said, "This is what I want you to do; get up and go do it."

For a moment, he forgot the music and looked around for the person who had interrupted his meditation. He searched the area carefully but saw only the organist at the console.

Could this be the voice of God? he thought. He thought hard and long. Suddenly, in an epiphany, he understood it was the voice of God. God knew he was at the crossroads in deciding if he should become a lay preacher. Here, he was being directed in another avenue of service for which he had no training or education. He was thrown into a dilemma. How could he go and play an organ when he never had a music lesson? He questioned himself and pondered the voice that gave the instruction. He returned home, and the voice continued to speak to him.

He did not tell any of his relatives about this experience for some time. One day, when he was overcome by the power of the message, he visited a retired organist from his church. He discussed the encounter with her, and she listened attentively. Then she said to him, convincingly, "That is the voice of God calling you to serve in that ministry in the church."

He said that he knew nothing about organ playing. However, he was interested in obeying the voice, but there were no music teachers in the village. Without hesitation, the lady said to him, "You can use my piano to practice on, and I will help you with a few lessons."

From that moment, everything began to fall into place, and he studied music. In a few years, he became the organist for his church and served in that capacity for forty-five years. He also taught several young people to play the piano and study music.

CHAPTER TWELVE
Leaving the Enclave

"You are so much stronger than what the world has ever believed you could be. The world is waiting for you to set it on fire. Trust in yourself." — **Clementine von Radics**

The day arrived, the day when Carlos would tell his mother that he was leaving home to work in North Sound, Virgin Gorda. He was still an adolescent, twenty years of age, but the time was ripe. His mother turned pale and remained silent for a few minutes before replying. Then she uttered, "God is everywhere, and He will protect and guide you. Keep close to Him and do not neglect to pray and read the Bible." It was not parting time, but sadness crept in as he began to think about home without him.

His only connection with the North Sound was through his mother's friends. He remembered the day when a boat named the "May Be" was launched in East End. The owners of the boat were from North Sound, and they had a festive time. As was mentioned before, it was the custom that when a large boat was launched, a picnic formed part of the celebrations. There were large quantities of food and drinks, and music filled the air. This boat launch remained in his memory because one of his mother's friends was a guest of his home. That same friend would be one of his caretakers several years after that boat launch. With that limited knowledge about North Sound, he accepted the offer to be the head of the school, hoping it would be a rewarding experience to live in a new environment.

He had to travel with furnishings for his apartment, and he had three weeks to get ready for that leg of his educational journey.

The journey to North Sound was on the government mail boat, which made a monthly visit to all the coastal villages where there were schools. Carlos boarded that boat on a bright sunny morning, and off he went to his new home. He felt like he was uprooted, but he wanted to launch out into deeper waters professionally. The mail boat berthed at the jetty in Gun Creek, North Sound, and everyone disembarked. The doctor, the nurse, the manager of the village school, and other government officials paid their monthly visits. It seemed to him that the community looked forward to the visit of the mail boat because the village postmistress, the local constable (auxiliary police), and others collected packages assigned to them from central administration in Road Town. In the middle of the busy hour, his landlord came to escort him to his apartment, which he would call home for the next three years. Suddenly, he heard a loud shout from a female onlooker standing on a nearby hillside crying out:

> *I hear dem sad at dey was senning a man teacher to de skool. Tis dat likkle boy! De children will soon fix he up.*

He was amused by her comment because he knew she would soon "swallow her words."

The first night in North Sound was eerie—the strange voices, strange chatter and laughter, familiar and unfamiliar sounds from insects pealing forth the music of the night at various pitches and beats. It sounded like an untuned orchestra without a conductor. During the first few days, the neighborly greetings overwhelmed him so much that he soon felt like he had lived in that village for several weeks. Everyone came to meet the new teacher, but the official welcome was given during the Sunday morning worship in the Methodist church. This was his first meeting with people from throughout the village, an initiation into the community. The village school was housed in the same Methodist church building. He was able to examine his workplace-to-be for the next few years. The community expected him not only to be head of the school but also to help the church to grow. This was familiar to him because the school he left behind was also housed in a church where he had been active.

The first day on the job was a new experience for Carlos. This was his first appointment as a manager of an organization, and to make matters even more difficult, he was not within reach of any senior associate if he needed assistance. There was no telephone, no television, no Facebook, no Twitter, no Instagram, no WhatsApp, only a letter that could take days or weeks to reach its destination. His staff greeted him cordially, and the students saluted with trepidation. They were curious to learn what kind of person he was and wasted no time in testing his endurance and resilience. The student body was one of the best that he would meet throughout his career. The students lagged behind other students in the territory because of limited educational opportunities. It was an opportunity for him to raise the level of student outcomes and help them to qualify to enter secondary school. Of course, many of the students who qualified could not attend secondary school because it meant living away from home. There were few boarding facilities, and the price was prohibitive for many of the parents. Even with government subsidies, it was difficult for them.

Two women, his mother's friend Mrs. Ura George and Mrs. Adina Rhymer looked after his welfare as if he were their son. His bonding with the community progressed rapidly and smoothly, and he soon became a friend of everyone in the village. It was a challenge to adjust to the many behavioral patterns, but he kept the focus on his mission and stuck with his religious values. Looking back today at the ease with which the boys learned to play string instruments—guitar, banjo, and ukulele—it compares favorably with the ease with which today's youths learn to use smartphones, iPads, and computers.

The senior citizens in the village were excellent storytellers. Oral tradition was strong in the village. Many of the residents lived in other countries for decades before returning home to retire. They brought with them a wealth of experience in trading, sailing, culinary art, carpentry, masonry, joinery, and instrumental music. He listened to the stories from those who lived on the Dutch island of Aruba and worked in the oil refinery. Others had emigrated to the Dominican Republic to work in the sugar industry, and many others had emigrated to the United States and worked in various industries before returning home. A few spent their lives sailing on cargo ships across the Atlantic Ocean. Those stories enriched the culture of the community. He found these seniors to be valuable resources and arranged for students to interview them from time to time. The results of these interviews provided meaningful topics for classroom discussions and student compositions.

One of his neighbors, the husband of his landlady, a very tall stately giant of a man who was over seven feet tall and wore size-14 shoes, had spent a great amount of time sailing the Atlantic. He told Carlos how, on one voyage, a severe storm caught the ship on which he was sailing at the harbor mouth of Portsmouth, England. The storm was so severe, the captain could not get the ship into port. It was impossible to turn back, and they were about to perish. At that point, he asked the captain's permission to take the ship into the harbor. The captain gave him permission, and he did so successfully to the amazement of all on board. He was honored for his skills and bravery. Since that adventure, he has been using his experience to motivate and encourage young people.

Carlos was hungry to learn more about those senior citizens. The following is an excerpt from an interview with Mr. Ray, a farmer, and Mr. Dan, a retired engineer from an oil refinery.

Carlos: "Greetings gentlemen, thank you for sharing some of your knowledge and experiences with me." Mr. Ray: "Nice to talk with you and get some of your knowledge, too." Mr. Dan: "Young man, tell something. Who is your father?" Carlos: "My father's name was Earl." Mr. Dan: "I met him many times with your grandfather in Road Town and in St. Thomas. I also met him that day when we launched *The May Be* in East End. Is your mother a Durante from Salt Island?"

Carlos: "That's correct." Mr. Dan: "What can we do for you today?" Carlos: Turning to Mr. Dan. "What was school like when you were a boy?" Mr. Dan: "We did not have any school like what these children have today. I had to work with my father from young, and when he died, I had to take care of my sisters." Carlos: "But you read the Bible well in church on Sunday." Mr. Dan: "I taught myself to read. I went to a little school run by a woman named Miss Dolly. Poor Miss Dolly did not know much, but she taught us our ABCs and good manners. She was a strict woman. Then, when I started sailing, I learned a lot from the people I met. I bought books and taught myself. I got some knowledge about arithmetic from Miss Dolly, and I built it up. Oh, Miss Dolly, bless her soul." Mr. Ray: "Dan, you forget how Mr. Higgs used to teach us the Bible in Sunday School? Poor Mr. Higgs did his best. We were cut off from the outside world up here. I heard the old folks say when the first airplane fly over the place, everybody ran to hide. One old man named Jimmy asked them if they were 'fraid of a 'hallelujah bird.'" Mr. Dan: "Yo right Ray. That must have been a fright. I ain't flying in no plane. Not a man get me up dere in God sky. When yo get way from dere tis down yo comin." Carlos: Shifting the conversation. "Who own all that hillside land?" Mr. Ray: "Boy! Dat's undivided property. The family have land up dere but dey did not divide it. Dey want it to stay in the family. My family own one hundred acres of dat lan." Carlos: "Would you sell me piece of that land?" Mr. Ray: "I can't sell any because it's family lan." Carlos: "Mr. Dan, what about you? Do you own a lot of land like Mr. Ray?" Mr. Dan: "My family has some lan, yes, but not a lot like Ray. My share belongs to my children." Carlos: "I see. So you won't sell me a house plot?" Mr. Dan: "If yo marry one of the girls from up here, I might." Carlos: Switching from Mr. Dan's remark. "Let us talk about fishing. Both of you set fish pots. Where do you sell your fish when you have a large catch?" Mr. Ray: "We go to the valley to sell fish and sometimes to Road Town." Carlos: "Do you love fishing?" Mr. Ray: "I love it, but it is too hard. Sometimes you go out all day, and you don't get enough to cook a pot. Other times you get a lot of fish. I thank God for giving us fresh food every day." Carlos: "Mr. Dan, tell me a little about your work in the oil refinery in Aruba." Mr. Dan: "That was hard work, but it paid off. We worked on three eight-hour shifts, so you were kept busy all the time. I worked with the engines, and you had to keep them clean and ready to run all the time. I enjoyed my years down there. A lot of other men from Tortola went down there too. One thing I come back with was a burning desire to get a school open here. We fought for it until the government and the church open a school for our children." Mr. Ray: "Boy, we had to fight hard. Dem people in Road Town did not care about us, so we had to show them who we were. One time, the Methodist minister came up to give communion. He wooder been dere standin til now. Not a soul study he. We show who we were. No school, no communion." Carlos: "What a thing! That poor minister! You all treated him badly." Mr. Ray: "Dey treated us worse. Bet dey listen after dat." Mr. Dan: "Me Boy, we doon make joke up here. If yo treat us good, we will treat you good. If you treat us bad, we do the same." Carlos: "I enjoyed speaking with both of you. I hope we can have another appointment soon. Thank you for your time, and enjoy the remainder of the day." Mr. Dan: "Thank you for helping our children. They are our future." Carlos: "Bye."

Carlos Developed lifelong friendships with the people of North Sound. He bonded with some of his lost relatives through his paternal grandfather's brother, who migrated from Anegada to North Sound. He was able to verify what his grandfather told him about those relatives. That discovery gave him a feeling of being home. The bonds he developed have continued to the present. He will always remember those years when he lived in North Sound.

Carlos gave a glimpse into his relationships with his mother, siblings, and the enclave while he resided in North Sound. If he was lucky, he could make monthly contact with his family. Transportation was poor. Perhaps he would take a boat trip at the end of the month to Road Town to collect his monthly salary. Every transaction was carried out manually, as there were no electronic banking facilities like today. That visit would normally be for a day, but on a few occasions, it would be extended for a weekend. Any prolonged contact with the enclave would occur during his vacation. He found his visits more positive and cordial than when he resided there permanently. The two women—his mother and his paternal grandmother—who contributed most to his success were always anxious to hear about his adventures. The visits were invigorating, energizing, and motivating. Those women always had plenty of advice to give him, and he had to listen to them even if he disapproved of their intrusions into his life. He knew they meant well, and, with that in mind, he gave them the respect they deserved. Their advice served him well in future years when he was faced with many challenges.

• • •

Above Round Rock

A frequent location discussed inside the enclave was "above Round Rock." Round Rock was the last island in the British Virgin Islands archipelago that the boats passed on their way to the more southerly Leeward Islands.

It referred to the last visible sight of the boat as it sailed beyond the horizon into the Caribbean Sea. Round Rock was, and still is, for people of Carlos's generation—those born during World War II and before—the dividing line between the cultures of the British Virgin Islands the Leeward Islands. Round Rock had also become a symbol of division between the better-educated people from the Leeward Islands and the less educated people of the British Virgin Islands.

During the first half of the last century, most senior civil servants and senior teachers, including principals, came from the Leeward Islands. There was free movement of people among the islands comprising the Leeward Islands Federation. Over time, the phrase "above Round Rock" signified superiority. Anyone or anything from "above Round Rock" was accepted without question. Even with the growth of education in the British Virgin Islands, the population still believed that anyone who came from "above Round Rock" was better prepared for a job. Tensions are still present in relationships between down islanders and British Virgin Islanders. The fertile soil for that thinking is found in the hearts and minds of some British Virgin Islanders who degrade their own people in favor of outsiders. Carlos had seen this in the enclave and in the wider community. He had seen it in purchasing real estate, in hiring and promoting public servants, as well as in other transactions.

The day came when Carlos was selected to go "above Round Rock" to attend teachers' college. There was a myth among people throughout the Leeward Islands that the size and power of one's brain were commensurate with the size of one's island community. He also discovered that some of the laborers at the college expected "small island" students to perform at a lower level than students from the larger islands. Carlos did not accept this attitude. He had always respected everyone as equal because each is God's creation. He believed that individual differences should be assets in building a better world, but many use them to highlight and fortify the baser behaviors of humankind.

Carlos viewed attending teachers' college as an opportunity to enhance his cognitive, affective, and psychomotor skills. It was an opportunity for him to spread his wings and view the world through the eyes of great writers. He used it to reflect on his future life in the classroom. It was one of those times when he reflected on "providence in his purpose." He asked himself questions like: would he be able to make a difference in the life of a young person who had no parents to guide them? Would he be able to help some youth who fell through the cracks in society and are struggling to get up? For him, education was the preparation in the dressing room for that stage of life. Could he live up to that?

The lessons he learned while growing up in the enclave colored his life and who he would become. Think about other people, lend a helping hand, help somebody every day, give of your best to the master, be kind, be honest, be fair to all, do not put any stumbling block in anyone's path, greet everyone with a smile, be content with what you can achieve honestly, protect the weak and less fortunate. These are some of the lessons that he learned and wanted to pass on to his students. What better place to reflect on these than teachers' college? This was a golden opportunity to refocus his path of his purpose. This period of preparation was rewarding.

He returned home better equipped to continue his journey as a teacher. That preparation enabled him to face what he would meet in his profession. Soon after he returned home, he was assigned to the Methodist School in West End. In many ways, it was like the schools at East End and North Sound. It was housed in the Methodist chapel and located on the outskirt of the village in a lonely little valley the local people called "Jumbie Ghut." There were no houses in sight from the church. The school community comprised the inhabitants of the valley Monday through Friday and the church community on Sunday. It was not unusual for the principal during the week to give the sermon on Sunday. In this tranquil setting, with the noise from the wild creatures and the few pedestrians passing through, West End school was nested.

At the time of Carlos's appointment, he was told by the manager and other government officials that discipline at the school was very poor and he should take the opportunity as a challenge. Indeed, the school was a rough community. Many of the senior boys challenged him in size and physical strength. The staff was afraid of those big boys, and so they influenced the behavior of other students. Carlos introduced all possible disciplinary measures, with few results, during the first three months. One day, he learned that six boys had planned to ambush him as he rode his bicycle away from school. He got all the details of the ambush from his clandestine informants, and he waited until they were secured in their hiding place before he went riding down the road. Everyone who knew about the plot waited anxiously to hear the outcome. For him, it was a turning point in managing the school. He was not going to allow that defining moment to be a defeat. He was going to teach these boys a lesson, and that he did. As soon as he arrived adjacent to the hideout, the leader jumped out and ran toward the bicycle. Carlos accelerated and ran the bicycle into him, knocking him to the ground, and then continued his journey. He did not look back at the scene. He heard when he returned to the school that the group fled when they saw their leader on the ground. On his return to the school from lunch, the school was so quiet, one could hear a marble dropped on the floor. He did not ask for that quietness. It was a quiet of fear, anxiety, expectation, and fright.

The news of the failed plot and the bruised leader had spread throughout the school. Carlos did not discuss the incident nor punish the perpetrators. The news spread that he was a force to be reckoned with, so all the students, including those boys, settled down to work. He used that opportunity to channel those boys' energy into fruitful activities to build their character. He gave them positions of responsibility, which they embraced, to improve the school environment. They became his friends. For the past half a century, the friendships have been kept alive with greetings, smiles, laughter, and retelling the story of the ambush. They have been trying all those years to find out why he did not punish them. Outside the life of the school, living and working in West End was a strong contrast to North Sound. The geography of West End is different from, though similar to, North Sound, each with a mountain range. West End has been a port of entry for various types of boats as well as a passenger ferry terminal for passengers from the US Virgin Islands. It has been a commercial port for many decades, and life was lived at a faster pace than at North Sound. Of course, there were similarities to North Sound. Many senior citizens had traveled to, and worked in, other countries and had returned home to retire. The parents showed similar interest in their children's education. The children who attended the school came from different areas. Carlos discerned three subcultures based on five factors:

a) Skin color
b) Educational achievement
c) Economic circumstances
d) Heritage
e) Religion

These factors were reflected in the behavior patterns of the students and adults alike. He quietly adjusted to this diversity because similar traits existed in the enclave where he grew up. For example, in the enclave, a family could buy a pew in the local church, and only members of that family could occupy it. He was also familiar with the ways people responded to the color of one's skin. The more "milk in the coffee"—that is, the fairer your skin—the higher you were placed in society. Such prejudices have weakened with time but have not disappeared. The intolerance of discrimination has forced these attitudes underground, but they have not died. These behavior patterns were present in the West End community, and the challenge for him was to treat everyone equally.

He got involved in community life and started a company of the Boys Brigade, which was attached to the Methodist church. It provided some meaningful activities—educational, spiritual, physical, and social—for male youths. He was keen on church music, and since the church did not have an organist, he served in that position for the duration of his stay in West End. He also discovered many maternal relatives he had never met, although his mother had told him about them. Transportation to and from West End, and even within the areas where students lived, was difficult to access. There were only a few private vehicles on the rough roads, and public transportation was not available. There was no telephone or television, but radio use was increasing. In this setting, the discovery of his relatives was a social oasis. Many of the relationships he developed are still alive today after more than half a century has passed.

The next leg of Carlos's professional journey took him to Cane Garden Bay for one year. The physical conditions under which he worked were similar to those at North sound and West End. The school was housed in the Methodist chapel, and the pastor of the church, like the other two schools, was the manager. The school operated jointly between the Methodist church and the government. The government financed the operations of the school and controlled the curriculum.

He arrived in Cane Garden Bay without fanfare. The people in this village were close-knit and different from the inhabitants of West End. They were friendly and kind but made rare appearances in public places in the village. They greeted him warmly but cautiously, something he had to overcome early to make any progress in the school. The land rivalry, which was characteristic of West End, was very present in this village. The first day at school was pleasant as he got to know the staff and the students. Most of the staff had worked at the school for several years, so they were familiar with the school's culture, something he had to learn. The following few days were spent planning for the school year, taking care to build on what his predecessors had accomplished.

The school was situated at the edge of one of the most beautiful beaches in the British Virgin Islands. The public highway separated the school from the beach property. The azure water, with waves breaking idly along the shore, boats sailing in and out of the harbor, visitors swimming and tanning on the beach, all served to distract the students from their studies. In the near distance, just two miles away, one could see the sister island of Jost Van Dyke lying in the confluence of the blue Caribbean Sea on the southern shore and the Atlantic Ocean washing its northern shore. There is a period every year when large Atlantic waves show no mercy, driving away the tranquil atmosphere and tearing up the beach with a vengeance. Sometimes, the damage is severe, causing businesses along the beach to close. The residents took precautions before this season of destruction. They could never predict the severity of those roaring groundswells. That was one of nature's secrets.

This natural phenomenon provided students with opportunities to study some physical geography as well as geological characteristics of the area. The resilience of the residents in recovering from the damage was admirable. It offered an opportunity for studies in disaster management, although that term was not used at that time. Periodically, the school would permit teachers to conduct classes on the beach. This attracted criticism from some of the parents, who believed learning should take place within the walls of the school. This view no longer prevails among the parents.

Carlos continued his research by interviewing and holding discussions with senior citizens. Many of them had wide and varied experiences of the sea. Many had lived in other countries and returned home to retire. Among them were a few very experienced sea captains, whose stories were always compelling and revealing. Even when their stories revealed their struggles, disappointments, tears, and losses, there was always a thread of hope running through all of them. They fought to be overcomers, and they were successful. They saw situations as temporary. They believed the sun, the rain, and the rainbow would continue to give hope.

More than half a century has passed since Carlos had these experiences. Many of the prophetic expressions made by these sages have been fulfilled. One theme that illustrates this was the isolation of the villages from one another. Anyone who visited those villages during that period could perceive specific characteristics in each area. The stories always echo a strong sense of unity, which was to come through better communication. Perhaps if these sages were to return from their graves, they would denounce the abuse of electronic communication and laugh at our dependence on vehicular transportation rather than walking short distances. They certainly would despise our dependence on imported foods rather than cultivating crops to supply our needs.

His life has been richer because he lived and worked in North Sound, West End, and Cane Garden Bay. Those three episodes form part of his providential journey and the discovery of his purpose on earth. He visits these places periodically to worship and celebrate festivities and to share in cultural activities. Living in these areas were epiphanies in becoming a servant leader. He saw service as his highest calling. He was not the same person when he returned to the enclave, and he never took up permanent residence there again.

CHAPTER THIRTEEN
Providence in Action

"Do what you feel in your heart to be right, for you'll be criticized anyway." —**Eleanor Roosevelt**

Carlos believed that God was always with him. It was God who spared his life in each of the following accidents. God sent his angels to protect him and gave him the assurance that he was on the right track in the service of humankind.

The first four accidents occurred at sea. Carlos and his father went fishing in a rowboat and were returning from Camanoe Island. His father decided to row through a narrow channel in the reef stretching from Little Mountain on Beef Island to Lloyd's Estate on Tortola. The Atlantic swells, locally called groundswells or ground sea, were breaking over the reef with fury and smashing anything in their path. The fishermen had a theory that if you count seven swells break on the reef, there would be a small window of calm. During this window, one could row through the channel quickly before the swells begin to break again.

Carlos and his father rowed swiftly through the channel, but they were not swift enough as one heavy swell rolled in and caught the boat. The thing to do at that time was to keep the boat straight and allow it to ride on the wave. Carlos was inexperienced in performing this skill, and he allowed the wave to break over the side of the boat. The boat filled with water, and everything that could float was out in the open sea. Had the next wave caught them, they would have been seriously hurt. They were fortunate that they were not thrown out of the boat. That was the hand of God guiding them because Carlos became so frightened that he remained frozen for a few minutes, helpless as the wave broke over his head. His father became nervous and began to tremble.

They gained enough courage to get the boat inside the reef in calm waters. The task was to bail all that water out of the boat by hand. It was exhausting work, and Carlos was tired at the end of that ordeal. They had to collect all the items that were floating around before they continued their homeward journey.

Carlos's father was angry and accused him of being incompetent and had failed to learn what he was taught. He even threatened to punish Carlos when he reached home. That never happened. On hearing the story, his mother accused his father of nearly drowning her child. He tried to convince her that the fault was Carlos's, but she flatly refuted his arguments by reminding him that "shortcuts lead to hell."

On another occasion, while he was still a young teenager, he accompanied his Uncle Emile to harvest fish from his fish traps. They had a bountiful catch and headed off to Road Town to sell fish. They were traveling in a small sailboat named *The Lily*. The market was good that day, for his uncle sold his fish in record time. They then did some shopping for groceries and were ready to sail for East End by midday.

Everything was going well, the breeze was gentle, the waves were small, and the boat glided over them smoothly. It was a very relaxing atmosphere, and even his uncle, who was at the tiller, seemed relaxed. Yet, it appeared that his relaxed mood interfered with his vigilance. Near Baughers Bay, just off where Caribbean Sailing is situated (it was not built at that time). A "hull wind," the name sailors gave to a heavy, isolated gust of wind, appeared suddenly and filled the sails with too much pressure. The wind listed the boat on its side until water began to fill the bilge. Carlos slackened the jib, and his uncle slackened the mainsail, but it took a while before the boat responded to the release of pressure from the sails. By the time the boat regained an upright position, it was more than half full of water. Carlos was too terrified to do anything, and his uncle was shaken by the ordeal. When it was all under control, Carlos could only offer a prayer of thanks to God for his survival. He believed that God had sent an angel to rescue them. His mother was patiently waiting for Carlos to return with some fresh fish for the evening meal. When he told his mother what had happened to them, and that he had lost the groceries, she simply said, with tears in her eyes, "My poor child."

He often wondered why his mother cried, but she never told him.

These two accidents increased Carlos's courage on the sea and helped him to become a better sailor.

A third challenge on the sea occurred in December 1956. Carlos made a trip to St. Croix on a small sailboat named *The Safety*, captained by the famous village captain Edward Frett. It was the week before Christmas, and the captain had planned to return home two days before Christmas Eve. Unfortunately, a heavy gale came down from the north, the direction for the homeward journey, and the boat could not sail. The captain waited for two days, but the gale increased in intensity. On the morning before Christmas Eve, the captain called everyone to a meeting and announced he was sailing that day. He had no intention of spending Christmas in St. Croix. Everyone feared the decision, but followed his instructions.

The Crucians said he was crazy to leave land, but he had a well-thought-out plan. Everyone was asked to eat a good breakfast because that would be the only meal for the day. Everything was strapped to the boat so that nothing could be washed overboard. Each person was commanded to tie a rope around his waist and fasten it to the mast so that if one was accidentally washed overboard, he could be rescued easily. When everyone was ready, the captain reduced the amount of sail he would use on the boat and tied the remainder firmly so that it would not get loose with the wind. The boat left St. Croix with waves breaking over it, and that continued for the forty-mile journey across the channel to the British Virgin Islands. The wind was blowing from the north where the boat was headed. The captain took a northwest course instead of northeast and ended up near St. Thomas, west of Tortola. When he sailed into Road Harbour, all the people came out to see who that captain was who braved that gale.

Carlos was drenched with seawater by almost every wave. He had never experienced anything like that in his life. He felt the assurance that God was with them, and he believed in the ability of the captain. He felt energized by the captain's bravery. It was a lesson in perseverance that he never forgot.

The following passage from *Psalms 107, verses 23-32*, had an indelible influence on Carlos's love for the sea:

> *Some went down to the sea in ships, doing business in the mighty waters; they saw the deeds of the Lord, his wondrous works in the deep. For he commanded and raised the strong wind, which lifted up the waves of the sea. They mounted up to the heavens, they went down to the depths, their courage melted away in their calamity, they reached and staggered like drunkards, and were at their wit's end. Then they cried out to the Lord in their trouble; he brought them out from their distress, he made the storm be still, and the waves of the sea were hushed. Then they were glad because they had quiet, and he brought them to their desired haven. Let them thank the Lord for his steadfast love, for his wonderful works to humankind. Let them extol him in*

the congregations of the people and praise him in the assembly of the elders.

Carlos reflected on the power and majesty of God as the waves tossed the little boat he was in, as well as the big ships on the ocean, and then raced for the coastline like an angry bull. As the vessels bounced around like driftwood in the sea, the sailors also stumbled to and fro, and sometimes lost heart in the presence of the stormy sea. After the storm came the calm, which speaks of the love of God and his caring spirit for humankind. The calm speaks to His power to answer prayers and protect His children.

The fourth sea incident occurred when Carlos was traveling from Road Town to East End on a cargo boat named *The Bells of St. Mary*. This boat was built in East End by Claremont Davies. He recalled the day when this boat was launched. Boat launching was a festive occasion, as mentioned earlier. The larger the boat, the greater the celebration, and *The Bells of St. Mary* was a large boat. Her launch attracted people from Road Town, West End, Carrot Bay, Cane Garden Bay, and Fahie Hill. It was a picnic in grand style. This journey from Road Town was Carlos's first trip on the boat.

When the boat left Road Town, there was a steady breeze blowing from the southeast, and all seemed well. The sails were hoisted, the anchor raised, and everyone on board was in a jolly mood. A local saying goes, "Merry bird the cat eats." Little did the people on that trap know that the cat would soon eat them. The boat made all the turns as it sailed towards East End. When it reached the vicinity of Hodges Creek, it sailed north from Peter Island. On nearing the land, the captain gave orders to turn about and change course. The Bells of St. Mary refused to change course. The sailors did everything they knew. They lowered the sails, but the boat refused to respond to the rudder. Everyone panicked. The boat was nearing shipwreck on a reef when the captain gave orders to lower the anchor.

That failed to stop the boat, and it dragged the anchor and ended up on the reef. There was Carlos, shipwrecked. He quickly jumped into the water to escape any injury if the boat was knocked over by the breaking waves. The sailors and the passengers escaped with bruises and cuts, but there were no life-threatening injuries. Carlos swam for a quarter of a mile to reach land, leaving all his belongings behind to the mercies of the waves. He gave priority to saving his own life.

When the story of the shipwreck reached the village of East End, people had several explanations for the mishap. Some said the rudder was too small for the boat; others said the boat had evil spirits on board, and they took control of the boat. Carlos was also interested in the reasons for the accident. He was thankful that he was alive and only sustained minor injuries. When he told his mother the story, she showed signs of distress and sighed, then she prayed silently. The only verbal response he heard from her was, "God watches over his children." He continued to believe that God had a special purpose for his life, and these experiences were part of his preparation for that purpose.

Carlos also had two encounters on land and two in the air, which strengthened his belief that he had a special purpose in life. The first on land occurred sometime after he had purchased his first car, a Volkswagen Bug. The day on which he would have an unprecedented experience began quietly. Everything was progressing smoothly. On his way to work, his world changed. A large truck transporting gasoline ran into his Bug. It was like a lion and a mouse in comparison. His vehicle was seriously damaged, and he received a heavy blow in the chest but was not unconscious. He was taken to the hospital for examination and remained there for twenty-four hours under observation. His physical injuries were not as traumatic as his emotional bruises. The trauma lasted a few days before he was able to return to work. He was thankful to God that his life was spared.

The following account was even more devastating for Carlos. The day was rainy, and he wanted to go home. He was working in West End and decided to hire a vehicle to carry him to East End. The journey was fifteen miles, and on well-paved roads would have taken about an hour because of the hilly terrain. However, the roads were rocky and unpaved, and the journey would take a much longer time. Soon after starting, he realized that the driver was under the influence of alcohol, and his judgment at certain points on the road was not very comforting. Still, he tried to endure the rough ride even though he was scared sometimes. The road was wet and slippery in some places, making the trip even more uncomfortable.

The journey was successful until they reached Fort Hill. There was no coastal road in that area and below the road was a steep cliff jutting into the sea, ending with large black boulders with sharp edges carved by centuries of waves beating against them. The only guardrail along the road on Fort Hill was three strands of wire cable fastened to a few metal posts. When the jeep reached the top of the hill, the driver failed to make the turn to descend into Baughers Bay at the foot of the opposite side of the hill. The jeep jumped over the guardrail and headed for the rocks below.

Carlos saw death staring him in the face, and he became frozen in his seat. The two front wheels and the right rear wheel were hanging in the air, and the left rear wheel was hooked in the guardrail. Carlos was still frozen with fright below the cliff on those black boulders. In an instant, he decided to jump, not knowing how far he would roll down the cliff. Fortunately, he landed on his feet and did not slide down the cliff. Still trembling, he managed to crawl on his knees onto the road.

The driver, who was too frightened to say anything, came out of the vehicle and stared at Carlos. Both were in shock. They could only sit and try to compose themselves without saying a word to each other. After about two hours, Carlos managed to secure a ride with another vehicle and continued his journey home terribly shaken after that narrow escape.

When he reached his home, he collapsed on the floor as he stepped inside the door. He was unconscious and could not tell anyone what had happened. Everyone was worried and began to apply local remedies to help him regain consciousness. When he revived and shared his story with his mother and siblings, his mother chastised him for traveling in that type of weather. He could only thank God for protecting him another time.

The news of the accident spread quickly through the enclave, and Carlos was flooded with get-well wishes. His old friend King happened to be in the enclave at that time, and he came by to console him. They shared stories about their work during the time they were apart. Carlos took the opportunity to encourage King to allow God to direct his life. As usual, King was dismissive of the encouragement and changed the conversation to his success in business. Carlos rejoiced with him in his success but reminded him again it was God who enabled him to succeed. They met periodically during their short visit to the enclave and promised to continue their friendship to help improve life in the enclave.

God protected Carlos on the sea and on the land. Now he will share two of his experiences in the air as he traveled to other countries.

On this first occasion, he was returning home from a conference in Barbados. The flight took off well. The weather was conducive to a smooth flight, and everyone on board seemed to be in good spirits. When the plane was nearing Antigua, a sudden explosion startled everyone. The plane began to descend rapidly. This continued until the plane was only a few hundred feet above the ocean when it leveled off. There was complete silence, and not one individual said a word until the rapid descent ceased. At that time, the pilot gave some comforting words, but everyone was shaken up, some trembling with fright.

The only thing Carlos could do was to offer a prayer to God for deliverance. The pilot's message was not very comforting because everyone was concerned about survival. The plane limped into Antigua with a load of frightened folks thoroughly shaken up. The ground crew was on hand to rescue the passengers if necessary and give assistance where it was needed. It was a traumatic experience for Carlos.

To make matters worse for him, he had to continue on that plane to his destination. The airline authorities tried to assure all passengers that the problem was addressed and the plane was safe. Carlos was uncomfortable about continuing his journey on that plane. He tried to secure another flight, but none were available to his destination within twenty-four hours. In a melancholy mood, he continued his flight in faith, believing that God would take him home safely. The onward flight was comfortable, but Carlos listened to every sound from the engines. Whenever the pilot made any adjustment to the flight instruments and the rhythm of the engines changed, Carlos's adrenalin flowed rapidly, and his body quaked with anxiety. This happened a few times before the plane landed at his destination. It took some time for his blood pressure to return to normal, but he was glad to be safe on the ground. When he shared his ordeal with his family, everyone rejoiced with him in reaching home safely.

On another occasion, Carlos was flying from Prince Edward Island to New Brunswick, Canada, when he experienced an even-greater scare. After the plane was airborne for a while, it was caught in a cold front. Suddenly, the chatter, laughter, and merriment on the plane turned into screams and prayers as the plane began a rapid descent. In addition to the shrieks, the piercing cries, and prayers from the passengers, food and drinks were strewn all over the floor. When Carlos looked on the floor, and he saw milk running under his feet, he could only say: "Lord, if this is my call, take me home with you." With that, he closed his eyes and waited for what would happen. He cannot recall how long the plane was in rapid descent, but after what seemed to be the most frightening time of his life, the flight returned to normal. The pilot spoke during this turbulence, but everyone was too frightened to listen to his message. The plane finally landed in New Brunswick. All the passengers rejoiced as they marched briskly from the plane. Carlos knelt on the ground and gave God thanks for once again escaping from claws of death.

Carlos believed that everyone has some accidents in life and sometimes very narrow escapes. He hoped that by sharing these experiences, someone might be encouraged to face life with the hope that God would always be there to help them in times of need. He who worked miracles over two thousand years ago can still work miracles today. His love for His children is unconditional and is accessible by everyone who wishes to follow Him. There are angels hovering over you now.

The years ahead promised to be different from the twenty-five years of this memoir. The community is becoming more divided, self-centered, multicultural, and multinational. People are becoming less trustworthy, driven by intrigue and hate more than love and compassion. Carlos sees hope as a light that shines beyond the darkness of these forces. That sunshine beyond the rules of mortal eyes, that sunshine beyond what we can imagine, that sunshine beyond what we can comprehend now motivates him to reach for the top.

CHAPTER FOURTEEN
Carlos's Future Identity

"Do something today that your future self will thank you for." — **Sean Patrick Flanery**

In the preceding chapters, Carlos took us on a journey of his past and present life. Before ending this memoir, he will now reveal what he wishes to be in the future. He has shown his growth over twenty-five years as he faced tough times and overcame them, becoming stronger and better equipped to chart his future.

He has been able to relate to people of all ages, ethnicities, nationalities, and races. His greatest joy of achievement manifested itself when he was able to help a weaker person emerge from the shadows that had hidden him.

As seen earlier, he had a strong belief that God had special work for him to do, but it was his responsibility to strive to achieve his goals. He had the tools of knowledge, skills, attitude, desire, and willpower to shape his future life.

Shortly after his father's death when Carlos was sixteen, that work began to show up in ways he could not imagine. He felt strongly that his purpose in life was to serve anyone, anywhere, anytime, and decided to develop his future self—his new identity.

During his past life, he held on to the hope that his family would succeed and overcome the challenges of life. He knew it was difficult for them, and they would have to struggle much more than he had struggled because life was becoming more complex every day. He devoted a significant amount of time to prayer, seeking strength for them to overcome the dark forces, seen and unseen, that were at work in the enclave. These forces would have engulfed anyone who was not vigilant. There were strong elements of hatred, suppression, envy, back-stabbing, defamation, and the list goes on. It was not easy for anyone to navigate through these influences without becoming contaminated. Therefore, the individual needed the help of God to succeed.

Carlos also hoped that his friends would give more attention to the intangible things of life, those things that were grounded in the spirit of truth and justice, those things that would stand the tests of time. He never succeeded in getting them to view life as he did, but he never gave up on them.

His mother had always reminded him that "tomorrow will be better than today, so work as if you will live forever and pray as if you are going to die in the next moment."

She did not speak the words alone, but she demonstrated them in her actions. On several occasions, Carlos overheard her speaking to one or more of her friends, rebuking them for their lethargic approach to work. She would impress upon them that she did not have a lazy bone in her body, and she could not tolerate lazy people. She would impress upon them that she did not want a lazy child around her, and she was intent on teaching her children how to work for what they needed. Whenever his mother conversed with her friends, be believed that she was teaching them to be positive about life, to have faith in themselves, and they would succeed in what they were doing. They would overcome the obstacles that showed up as they journeyed through life.

Her faith in the future led him to have the same expectations. He believed that "hope springs eternal." When Jesus told his disciples to seek the Kingdom of God first, and all other things would be given to you (*Matthew 6:33*), that was a directive to live in hope. Throughout the Bible, God had given directions to people to have hope for a brighter, better tomorrow. Isaiah proclaimed this message in these words:

> *Those who hope in the Lord will renew their strength. They will soar on wings like eagles; they will run and not grow weary; they will walk and not faint. (Isaiah 40:31).*

Hannah lived in the hope that God would open her womb so that she could have children. She prayed fervently for that to happen, and when the time was ripe, God gave her a son whom she named Samuel. This story can be found in the *Book of 1 Samuel, Chapter One*. Jeremiah also confirmed God's guidance for those who had hope for tomorrow:

> *I know the thoughts I have for you to give you a future and to give you hope. (Jeremiah 27:11).*

The apostle Paul picked up this theme in his epistle to the Romans when he wrote:

> *Be transformed by the renewing of your mind, that you may prove the good acceptable and perfect will of God. (Romans 12:2).*

These passages also remind us that our mind is important in our search for the hope that God had given us through His Son. He sent His Son to die on the cross for the sins of humankind so that everyone can have the assurance of inheriting the Perfect Will of God. That was the ultimate hope of Carlos's life. He hoped that one day, through the daily renewing of his mind by the word of God, eternal life would become a reality. It would be a hope fulfilled.

Until that time comes, he was a work in progress as a human being. He was still in the potter's hands, being shaped and remolded daily. He has shown his past and present identities, and now he addresses his future. Having discovered his purpose on earth, he had to decide what he envisaged his future self on earth to be in order to fulfill that purpose. This meant that he would have to change his identity narrative from what he had become to what he can become. He decided to invest in his future self and change his narrative. He would have to prepare to face uncertainties and change as well as embrace new learning and associated failure. He would have to propel himself forward by this motivation to create a new identity, a new self. He would not be defined only by what he had achieved but also by the prospects for new achievements. He would look around the bend and beyond the horizon.

Just when Carlos was thinking about this new thrust in his life, his guardian angel was at work for him and revealed the path. He was teaching a course to a group of young teachers-in-training. This course was sponsored by the University of the West Indies, and the supervisor visited periodically to evaluate the students' progress.

On this visit, his supervisor suddenly confronted him with this question: "What are your plans for the future?"

Carlos was struck by the serious look on his supervisor's face and his piercing eyes.

"I have not decided on any plans," he replied.

"Young man," the supervisor said to Carlos, "you are wasting your time in this position. If you can bring those teachers to the level that I found them, I say you are wasting your time. You need to spread your wings and launch out into the wider world of academia. There are great possibilities for you out there."

Still awestruck, his mind spinning like a top, Carlos thanked his supervisor for the advice.

In a firm voice, the supervisor made this request of Carlos. "I would like a report on your progress in preparing to move out on my next visit."

Carlos had not been given such an ultimatum since the death of his father. Here he was confronted with this challenge from an unknown person. What triggered his interest in Carlos? It was an unusual experience. Except for his mother, grandmother, a few uncles and aunts, and two women, Alicia and Leah, he never met anyone so keenly interested in his advancement.

He thought about the encounter and pondered it day after day, but he did not take any action. He believed that as principal of an elementary school, he was fulfilling his purpose. When his supervisor returned, the first thing he did was request the progress report from Carlos. When he discovered that Carlos had not taken any action, he became angry and chastised Carlos as if he were his son. In that moment of chastisement, Carlos realized that his supervisor was only a messenger, but the message was coming from a more powerful source.

Carlos descended into a mood of penitence, and at that point, his supervisor mapped out a plan of action for him. His supervisor had done some research in the government and discovered that the government had been given many scholarships offers from other Commonwealth countries, but no effort was made to recruit candidates. He told Carlos about his discovery and directed him to apply for a Commonwealth scholarship sponsored by Canada.

Carlos's penitence led to conversion, and he accepted the plan that his supervisor had mapped out for him. He decided to pursue advanced studies in Canada and was awarded the scholarship. This was a step in changing his future identity narrative. It was commensurate with what he envisioned as his future self. All this came through the advice of his supervisor, who Carlos concluded was an angel in disguise. This experience increased Carlos's motivation to help others find and develop their new identity narratives to strive toward their new selves. He dedicated his life afresh to this mission for humankind. He set himself four goals for his future self:

1. To pursue advanced studies.

2. To aim for directorship of the education system.

3. To increase his involvement in community service.

4. To become a lay preacher in his church.

Carlos had reached the top of the career track that he had been following, and as part of defining his future identity, he proposed to change lanes. The shift from an elementary education career to a high school, post-secondary, and administration career meant pursuing related studies as part of the preparation. He devoted four years overseas to studies before reentering the education system. On his return, he was better equipped to be a trailblazer in education reform in his home country. That journey would be the subject of another memoir.

One of the immediate areas where the need was greatest was in the evaluation of student outcomes. The education system had evolved from the one handed down from Great Britain, and the essay as the main evaluation instrument was gradually being challenged by a new instrument: multiple-choice tests. He spent a significant amount of time studying this new evaluation instrument so that he would be equipped to lead his colleagues in this area.

When the Caribbean Examination Council became the chief external examining board for the Caribbean, it used this evaluation instrument in all its examinations. At that time, Carlos's colleagues in the Virgin Islands were well-prepared for the change.

Carlos also wanted to see secondary education expanded to the sister islands within the Virgin Islands archipelago. This was an objective he hoped to achieve and in keeping with the philosophy of inclusion that would characterize his new identity. He wanted students on the sister islands to have similar opportunities as those on the main island to attend high school on their home island. This education would be designed to meet workforce needs. At that time in the history of the territory, the economy was moving from predominantly agricultural to service-oriented. This transition was supported by the introduction of tourism as a new economic pillar. He also saw the need for students to be immersed in cultural activities in the education system to help them to increase their interest in national pride. He planned to pursue these activities as he attempted to define and expand his future identity.

He was confident that, as director of education, he would be able to effect meaningful growth at all levels of the education system—from preschool to tertiary, to meet the growing needs of the population. His community was changing rapidly through immigration, mainly from English- and Spanish-speaking countries in the Caribbean. This diversity would be an opportunity for him to introduce his inclusive philosophy. He wanted to see a community where everyone would feel welcomed and given opportunities for advancement.

Carlos also saw the need to be more involved in community development. This would continue an area of involvement in which he had been engaged since he was a teenager. When he discovered that there were no young musicians in training to replace the older generation nearing retirement from positions like church organist and leaders of youth organizations, he responded to that need. He introduced music classes for young people at his home. Many young adults benefitted from this opportunity. Thus, in developing his new identity, he would expand this area of service to meet the needs of a wider cross-section of the community. His aim would be to implement a program of instrumental music in the school curricula when he became director of education.

In keeping with his belief in the power of Providence in his life, he would render service to his people as a lay preacher in the Methodist Church of the Caribbean and the Americas. That lay ministry would enable him to reach out to thousands of people in various ways. He would be able to serve people from all walks of life and help them to find their identities. Hopefully, many of them would be motivated and empowered to give their best in the service of humankind. To all of them, he says to take action and invest in building your future identity, your future self.

I leave you with the words of Benjamin Hardy:

Destiny is not created by the shoes we wear but by the steps we take. Let's make the journey of life meaningful and memorable. It's your road and your road alone. Others may walk it with you but no one can walk it for you.

Finally, Carlos admonishes everyone:

Whenever trouble comes your way, let it be an opportunity for joy. For when your faith is tested, your endurance has a chance to grow, for when your endurance is fully developed, you will be strong in character and ready for anything. If you need wisdom, if you want to know what God wants you to do, ask him. . . . But when you ask him, be sure that you really expect him to answer, for a doubtful mind is as unsettled as a wave of the sea that is driven and tossed by the wind. (James 1: 2-6 NLT).

www.ingramcontent.com/pod-product-compliance
Lightning Source LLC
Chambersburg PA
CBHW071829080526
44589CB00012B/957